CHANGE, STRATEGY AND PROJECTS AT WORK

CHANGE, STRATEGY AND PROJECTS AT WORK

Roger Jones
and
Neil Murray

AMSTERDAM • BOSTON • HEIDELBERG • LONDON
NEW YORK • OXFORD • PARIS • SAN DIEGO • SAN FRANCISCO
SINGAPORE • SYDNEY • TOKYO
Butterworth-Heinemann is an imprint of Elsevier

The Open University

Published by Butterworth-Heinemann, an imprint of Elsevier
Linacre House, Jordan Hill, Oxford OX2 8DP, UK
30 Corporate Drive, Suite 400, Burlington, MA 01803, USA

in association with

The Open University
Walton Hall, Milton Keynes, MK7 6AA, UK

First edition 2008

British Library Cataloguing in Publication Data
A catalogue record for this book is available from the British Library

Library of Congress Cataloging in Publication Data
A catalog record for this book is available from the Library of Congress

ISBN: 978-0-7506-8944-1

For information on all Butterworth-Heinemann publications
visit our website at www.elsevierdirect.com

Typeset by Charon Tec Ltd., A Macmillan Company
(www.macmillansolutions.com)

Printed and bound in Hungary

This book forms part of an Open University course T226 *ICTs, change and projects at work*.
Details of this and other Open University courses can be obtained from the Student Registration
and Enquiry Service, The Open University, PO Box 197, Milton Keynes MK7 6BJ, UK:
tel. +44 (0)845 300 60 90, email general-enquiries@open.ac.uk, http://www.open.ac.uk

Contents

Contents

Contents

List of activities

List of figures

List of tables

Preface

This book aims to provide you with a working insight into the nature of change, the formulation of strategy and the implementation of change through projects in the workplace. We say insight because there is no intention to offer a text that would satisfy the professional change or project management specialist. There is an abundance of management books up to – and beyond – MBA level that separately address managing change, developing strategy and project management as specialist subject areas. In our book we aim to integrate these aspects – which in our view are too often treated as separate disciplines – in a coherent way. However, this is not just another academic 'text book', the focus throughout is on praxis, '... *the process by which a theory, lesson or skill is enacted or practised[sic].*'[1] Therefore, we aim to equip you with the knowledge, skills and techniques to help you apply what you learn in a practical way – and to learn from that experience.

A central assumption of this book is that all too often, people tasked with implementing change and those affected by it are not involved in the strategic analysis that preceded the implementation phase; moreover, they often do not understand how strategic objectives emerge from the analysis or the forces driving those objectives. It is our view that *everyone* within an organisation should have an awareness of the wider organisational context and the strategic planning process that gives their organisation direction and impacts on their careers. This entails not just passively receiving strategic objectives handed down from on high like the Ten Commandments, but really understanding the context within which these particular strategic objectives were

---

[1] http://www.encyclopedia.thefreedictionary.com/Praxis + (proces)

chosen. After all, we all need to be strategic at times in our personal lives, though we may not be aware of this – planning holidays, deciding where to go and how to get there, planning where we wish to live and how and where our children will be educated and so on.

Clearly, it is easier to achieve the necessary level of awareness and understanding in smaller organisations, but we believe that many larger organisations could do much more to empower their employees with knowledge about the change context and organisational strategy. The notion that change and strategy are things that can safely be left to 'senior managers' and specialist change managers and project managers is anachronistic in the era of globalisation. For organisations to survive, let alone prosper, in such a dynamic environment they must get the most out of their people in terms of energy, initiative and intellectual capital. Every employee should be encouraged to see themselves as a potential agent of change (a change agent) and be equipped with the knowledge, tools, techniques and *confidence* to suggest ways of improving personal and organisational performance.

Smart leaders within organisations know that it is often the people closest to the task who know how it could be performed more effectively. It is also our contention that, if people feel more included in their organisation's strategic planning process and are empowered to make suggestions for improvement, they will be more motivated and creative at work. It is this motivation and creativity that can lead to innovation, which is the lifeblood of all organisations in a rapidly changing environment.

So, this book is not aimed particularly at people with 'manager' in their role or mindset, though we all have something that we need to manage. Whatever our day-to-day role in the workplace, sports club and so on, you may sometimes find that you are the person best placed to pick up and run with a particular challenge or opportunity that change presents. You take on the role of the 'situational' manager or leader, when for a period you become the lead player, making the running and calling the shots. You need to be prepared for such opportunities when they arise – and even to seek them out.

This book will help you build your insight, knowledge, skills, competencies and other attributes that will help you to engage successfully with change, strategy and projects undertaken in the workplace. Your current responsibilities may already require some of these attributes though perhaps you are not fully aware of them or sufficiently confident should you be called upon to use them to create opportunities for yourself and your organisation.

The book starts by recognising that the rumblings of change are generally accompanied by a flurry of reactive activity along the lines of 'what can we do to head off this or make the most of that?' In this book we demonstrate how to take a more pro-active, systematic and rigorous approach to change, strategic planning and project working. Effective strategic planning is about analysing and anticipating change; analysing factors and trends that may have an impact, then planning, designing and finally implementing a strategy for survival and/or success. Implementing a strategy successfully frequently requires the development of a change programme which is invariably implemented through one or more projects.

Change can vary significantly in its nature, intensity and scale. We use the term 'programme' to refer to a comprehensive and more or less structured response to a change situation, which must address the strengths, weaknesses, opportunities and threats that may have been identified both within the organisation and in the external context in which the organisation operates.

From a practical standpoint a, change programme may require a multiplicity of projects to be carried out; each project representing a significant step forward towards the required outcomes of the change programme. Working through change programmes and the associated projects require skills that are highly marketable employability skills. At the end of this book we will review the skills, competencies and other attributes that need to be developed to improve your employability.

As you read this book you will see that analysing and managing change effectively is largely about establishing the aspirations of the organisation and the strategy needed to achieve those aspirations. However, it is all too easy to concentrate on the abstract notion of 'the organisation' and in the process forget that organisations are made up of people with different attributes, needs, motivations and aspirations. Taking into account the 'human' dimension of change is a crucial factor in any change programme or project.

Sometimes the exact outcome of a strategic change programme may not be precisely defined at the start because there are too many unknowns; sometimes the only 'known' is that significant change is required if the organisation is to prosper or perhaps survive. Planning to implement a change programme must therefore take this on board.

In project working there is a greater emphasis on defining as precisely as possible all factors concerned with attaining the required project outcome. Project working, therefore, has an increased focus on the technical and procedural aspects involved in introducing practical change – though, of course, human factors such as effective team working and individual and group behaviour are still crucial to a successful outcome.

After reading this book you should be in a strong position to contribute to the analysis, planning and implementation of change, whatever your day-to-day role entails, enabling you to carry through the associated practical workplace projects to achieve your organisation's strategic objectives and adding value to your organisation in the process.

Although an organisation may commission specialists to work at a strategic level, there is no substitute for employees actively supporting and engaging with the delivery of change in their workplace. A progressive organisation will encourage its employees to critically review workplace practices and introduce innovative improvements in order to keep the organisation relevant and competitive. Working carefully through this book will help you view the world through the eyes of a change agent or change leader as well as someone on the receiving end of change. Ultimately it should help you to create new opportunities for yourself and for your organisation.

How to use this book

This book is designed to be used in a variety of ways to suit particular audiences. It can be read as a narrative account of change, strategy and projects at work. It can also be used as a 'toolkit' containing tools, techniques, advice and guidance on how to go about analysing the organisational context, developing a strategic plan and managing a project. In this sense it is a 'how to' book with a practical application, which you can dip in and out of as required. However, the book also forms a central part of an Open University course that enables students to gain academic credit for demonstrating an ability to successfully apply the key concepts, tools and techniques contained herein to their own workplace. Readers who are pursuing this route will be guided by other course materials to study the text and apply the knowledge and skills acquired in a more systematic and coherent way.

Whichever way you intend to use this book we are confident that, having gained an understanding of change, the organisational context and strategic planning, you will be in a much better position to develop and plan a work-based project that improves the way you work and adds value to your organisation.

1 The nature of change

Introduction

Death and taxes, it is often said, are the only certainties in life; but to these must be added change. Change happens for a number of reasons, not least because humankind is inherently creative seeking to change the world, or at least part of it, for some economic, social or other perceived benefit. However, as well as opportunity, change can bring with it challenges, uncertainty and insecurity – so understanding what drives change and how to cope with it involve important life and work skills.

History provides many rich accounts of how people, organisations and nations have reacted to change throughout the centuries. In the contemporary world, globalisation – the increasing intensity, extent and complexity of interactions on a global scale – is driving change at ever greater speed and so we all need to learn how to live with change and meet the challenges it brings.

Change and innovation are closely linked. Innovation is about doing something new or doing something in a new way that creates value for an organisation, group or wider society. According to Luecke and Katz (2003)[1]:

> *Innovation … is generally understood as the successful introduction of a new thing or method … Innovation is the embodiment, combination, or synthesis of knowledge in original, relevant, valued new products, processes, or services.*

Innovation is crucial in creating a competitive advantage and even in non-profit making organisations there is an ongoing need to ensure that services, products and processes

---

[1] Luecke and Katz (2003).

are improved in innovative ways to avoid an organisation becoming stagnant, irrelevant and, therefore, dispensable. Of course, not all change initiatives will have innovative outcomes, but it is difficult to innovate if an organisation is averse to change.

Change is not an unfamiliar concept; in the context of this book it expresses how life will be somehow different tomorrow or, perhaps, in the months or years ahead. It can, however, evoke strong defensive reactions. To seek to secure that which is familiar, even if this means burying our heads in the shifting sands of change, is a common response. We may find temporary refuge by battening down the hatches, but where does safety really lie? Surely not by denying that the world is changing but rather by facing up to change and making the best of the challenges and opportunities that it creates?

Change affects us all periodically in our personal, social and working lives. We may find change, and the new challenges it brings, exciting or we may suffer diminished confidence in our ability to cope with new ideas, technologies, processes and the new ways of doing things. We may feel nervous and reluctant to abandon the ways we have always done things, especially when things have worked well – thus far!

How do you feel about change?

Sometimes change may have been anticipated but at other times it comes out of the blue. The consequences may be positive, such as being promoted at work, and at other times negative, such as when a close friend or family member dies. When change is unwanted, even when it is anticipated, we can experience a roller coaster of emotions, which may be traumatic depending upon the degree of change we are experiencing. Read through the box entitled *The coping cycle* and think about experiences you have had when you have undergone some significant change in your personal or working life.

The coping cycle

Table 1.1 identifies five phases that are characteristic of the way people react to change. Similarities can be seen whether the change is something that has been anticipated, such as a proposed change at work, or something that comes out of the blue, such as a serious illness or death.

Table 1.1 *The coping cycle*

Phase 1	Denial	Initial disbelief that a change is underway 'We have always done things this way' 'Why change, we are making a profit aren't we?' 'Don't change a winning team' 'We tried that before but it did not work'
Phase 2	Defence	Reality intrudes and people realise they must react. 'That's fine but it won't work in my area' 'I'd like to get involved but I have too much work to do' 'The theory is fine, but it won't work in practice'
Phase 3	Discarding	Moving on from the defensive stance 'Whether I like it or not, it is going to happen, so I had better…' 'Well here it is; we are committed to it; here's how I see it' 'I was giving that new machine a try, and do you know…?' 'I've been asked to join the group looking at x'
Phase 4	Adaptation	Experimenting and feeling the way forward 'We are still trying to get the new x to work' 'We are getting most of the output from the new x but I still think we need to…' 'We are never going to get x to work unless those so and so's in that department pull their finger out' 'I kept telling them that that was what we needed to do and finally they have done it'
Phase 5	Internalisation	What was the future state is now the current state. 'I was talking to x in the y department the other day about that customer order…' 'We are getting a group together to see whether we want to implement that software upgrade' 'That is one of the things I want to raise at my next review'

Source: *Adapted from Carnall (1999)*

An individual's perspective of a change can typically lead to variations in levels of self-esteem and of performance (which are closely linked) and these are likely to vary with time as the individual passes through the stages of denial, defence, discarding, adaptation and internalisation, as shown in Figure 1.1.

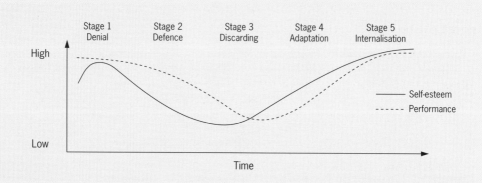

Figure 1.1 *The coping cycle: effects on performance and self-esteem*
Source: *Carnall (1999)*

Change is all about moving from an initial state to a new state. The initial state may be one in which we have felt comfortable for some time, being characterised by comparative stability, unchanging routines and a psychological state of relative satisfaction with things as they are.

When change happens the comfort ceases and a period of uncertainty begins where we may question the necessity of change and what it will mean for us. The transition between the old and the new states involves the movement away from the familiar but with little idea yet of what the future state holds. This is a period of instability, in which our response to change may be dominated by negative thoughts and concerns.

Some time afterwards, when the new state becomes the accepted normality, we may feel a period of psychological comfort returning as we learn to engage with the new order and the opportunities that accompany it.

In an organisational context change can be unsettling. The leaders in an organisation may understand that change is needed, but not necessarily what form it should take. In Chapter 2 we will be exploring how an organisation can work through this dilemma and determine its best way forward.

The metaphor of undertaking a journey is appropriate for both the individual and the organisation facing change. Read through the box headed *The journey metaphor*.

The journey metaphor

◆ Where are we now?

◆ Where do we need to get to?

◆ Are we heading in the right direction?

◆ What are the options along the way to help us to reach our destination?

The direction we should take (as an individual or as an organisation) will depend upon the starting point, our purpose (often referred to as the 'mission'), an idea of where we need to be – our destination (articulated as the 'vision') and how we can best plan and navigate our route and organise ourselves to get there. The options for getting to the desired future state will include the choice of route, the means of travel and how urgently arrival is required.

Proposed change is unlikely to be embraced enthusiastically by everyone from the start and so leaders and agents who are involved in introducing change need to be aware of the fluctuations in self-confidence, self-esteem and motivation that others can experience as they progress through the coping cycle.

Reading through the box headed *Change perceptions* you will see that change isn't easy because people often deny the need for change, preferring instead to stay within, or return to their own comfort zone. Even when there is a recognition that change is beneficial and an individual initially engages with change, early efforts can soon falter, as we all know from many abandoned New Year resolutions! This can be a corporate failing too. There are plenty of examples of organisations that have failed to change – even when faced with overwhelming evidence of the need to do so.

On the other hand, change can create a tremendous buzz leading to a sense of liberation and achievement when people realise that they are making a difference and that their contributions are being valued, perhaps for the first time. In the virtuous circle depicted in Figure 1.2, an increase in self-esteem is accompanied by an improvement in effectiveness, performance and enthusiasm. Developing people in this way is a worthy challenge for those championing the cause for change.

Change perceptions

Will I

- lose my job?
- be sidelined?
- have to work with new people I don't know or don't like?
- have to develop new skills, learn new things?
- have to move to a new location?
- be asked to do things I don't agree with?

I can't see the reason for change!

We've been through all this before!

Is this change for change sake – just another management fad?

For employees, change can present a period of doubt, uncertainty and possibly fear of the unknown. An individual may feel threatened as accepted work practices are challenged and their role in the organisation becomes uncertain. Employees may feel helpless because, despite brave words about participation from management, they feel

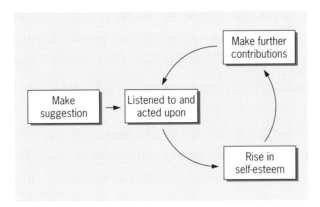

Figure 1.2 *Virtuous circle – self-esteem leading to improved performance*

that change is something that happens to them rather than something they can or want to contribute to. A new change initiative may well be seen as just the latest in a series of management fads.

The challenge for any organisation is to resolve these potential conflicts and mobilise its workforce to reach the destination and achieve the organisation's strategic vision. In an increasingly volatile and globalised world, it is this ability to manage change effectively that can separate industry leaders from the also-rans.

From a personal and career perspective, you need to be able to understand, and contribute to the implementation of change processes. You also need to be able to recognise and use the opportunities for personal and career development during times of change.

Next we will look at the types of change that can arise.

Different types of change

Developmental to transformational

Organisations routinely experience minor levels of change every day when, for example, orders are taken from new customers, employees join or leave, production schedules and processes are modified. These day-to-day occurrences do not generally create significant difficulties for organisations or the people involved in implementing them and they are usually dealt with in a routine manner. Our primary focus will exclude this level of change that we can accommodate routinely.

Significant change can though include that which is incremental in nature. Such change is often termed developmental change because it is usually planned to correct or enhance some existing aspect of an organisation; for example, when processes are significantly upgraded to meet required quality or safety standards. The introduction of specific new skills or perhaps more general up-skilling in an organisation could also be classed as 'developmental'. Continual improvement programmes often involve this type of incremental change.

Again, this level of change may be systematised into the normal way of working in many organisations, particularly in manufacturing industry. However, every so often, more significant change may become necessary. This is when the established ways of doing things become unsatisfactory or inadequate and major change is required to establish a new framework in our lives or work. In your personal life, for example, you would undergo major change in starting a family, changing career, or approaching retirement. Organisations may be forced into making significant changes for a variety of reasons, ranging from new competitors entering their markets to advances in the technology underlying their products or services.

This level of change is usually referred to as transformational change. Transformational change is a more fundamental form of change; one that cannot be handled within the day-to-day procedures of an organisation. In this type of change the organisation makes fundamental changes in the way it carries out its business under the influences of external or internal pressures. By its nature it can be more disruptive and worrying for the people involved in or affected by it, but it can also be an exciting and interesting opportunity for creativity and innovation to flourish.

It may be necessary to throw away the 'rule book' during such periods of transformational change. To complicate matters there could be disagreement about what is happening, what needs to be done or even about what the organisation should be trying to achieve. This transformational form of change will be the main focus in the following sections of this book, though you should appreciate that change is a continuum and particular episodes can fall anywhere between the extremes of developmental and transformational change. The unique opportunities and the potential disruption, uncertainty and risks can also vary considerably.

This would be a good time to work through Activity 1.1

Closed, contained or open?

Rationalising the need for change and working out how best to plan for it is important. Ralph Stacey (1996) distinguished between change episodes where there are varying levels of certainty:

◆ Closed change, where there is certainty about what happened, why it happened and what needed to be done.

◆ Contained change, where there is reasonable confidence about what happened, why it happened and what needed to be done.

◆ Open-ended change, where there is disagreement about what happened, why it happened and what needed to be done.

The degree of agreement and the degree of uncertainty can be represented as in Figure 1.3.

From the descriptions of closed, contained and open-ended change you should see that the approach to planning is dependent upon the type of change that is involved.

For closed change where there is general acceptance and agreement, the planning and management of the necessary change can be defined in some detail and to an agreed schedule. Where change is open ended and is undertaken in a context that is complex and uncertain, rigorous and detailed planning is likely to be difficult and less effective – though

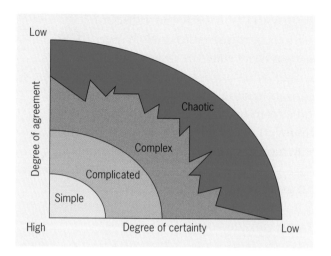

Figure 1.3 *Stacey agreement versus certainty matrix*[2,3]

planning the framework for change to happen is still essential. Here the change situations and the possible problems and solutions may not be predictable from the start. In complex situations, the creation of the future state can emerge as a consequence of the actions and interactions of those engaged in the change process. The skills of the change leader should focus upon the buy-in and engagement of all who are affected, so that solutions are proposed that meet the requirements of the adopted strategy without the change becoming inherently uncontrollable in the chaotic region of Figure 1.3.

The term 'emergent' is used to describe change that cannot be planned definitively and in detail from the start, but which emerges as things become clearer and possible solutions become evident. Emergent change, therefore, arises as a consequence of undertaking and engaging with the change process, rather than it being defined in detail at the start. However, for all types of change there will need to be a careful analysis of both the external forces at play as well as the internal resources available to the organisation to meet the challenge.

This would be a good time to work through Activity 1.2

---

[2] Stacey, R. (1996). *Strategic Management and Organizational Dynamics*, 2nd edition, London: Pitman.
[3] www.jiscinfonet.ac.uk.

Continuing waves of change

For some organisations, the pressure to change is now so relentless that it is desirable to develop processes and cultures that can deal with change that is ongoing throughout the organisation. It should be one of the aims of any change programme to make an organisation more receptive to future change as well as to the current change proposal. What this means in practice is that those involved in introducing change into an organisation, whether as managers, leaders or agents of change need to acquire the necessary skills to simultaneously cope with ongoing operational matters, whilst at the same time contributing effectively to change programmes. An organisation that can conduct its routine business efficiently whilst also introducing beneficial change is likely to thrive in a turbulent operating environment.

There are many examples of organisations where a 'continual improvement' approach has been adopted. However, here we are referring to continuing cycles of a higher level of transformational (rather than incremental) change. An organisation that can survive in this environment is amoeba-like in form, flexible in structure and fluid in its processes, enabling it to respond rapidly to new challenges even before they appear over the horizon.

These organisations are likely to want to leverage the most out of their staff, encouraging them, whatever their level of activity, to think 'outside the box', to think innovatively about potential change and to contribute their ideas to the organisation. The term 'learning organisation' describes such organisations where the approach to change is characterised by a continuous learning process.

Readiness to change – culture, power and politics

All organisations develop a distinct cultural identity which may become an asset or a liability during periods of change.

People within organisations are both influenced by and contribute to the organisation's established culture. You can certainly see and feel differences in cultures even when visiting them as outsiders or customers.

Culture in an organisation is sometimes expressed by 'the way we do things around here'. It is the result of shared norms, values and perceptions. It can be seen in the dress codes, the rituals that people engage in, the stories they tell and how they relate to work colleagues as well as others outside the organisation such as customers and suppliers.

An organisation's culture normally develops gradually and partly as a result of management 'design', partly as a result of the sector in which the organisation operates and partly as a result of employee experiences, historical anecdotes, and demographic mix of the workforce and so on. There may be variations of an organisation's culture within the groupings that make up an organisation. For example, IT departments are renowned for developing their own sub-cultures.

Figure 1.4, adapted from Johnson and Scholes (1999)[4] shows how the main elements of cultural identity interact to form the predominant cultural mindset that people share in an organisation.

The cultural identity of an organisation straddles the informal and the formal structure. Those who have formal power in an organisation may try to change the existing culture but within the informal structure there will also be those who have some power or influence and who will seek to sway actions or decisions in a self-interested way.

Whilst culture can help create a sense of belonging and shared destiny, it can also prove to be an obstacle to change especially where the existing culture is risk averse or if the change strategy is perceived by some to challenge prevailing group values. Where radical change is proposed, the achievement of cultural change may actually be a major objective of the proposed change.

[4]Johnson and Scholes (1999).

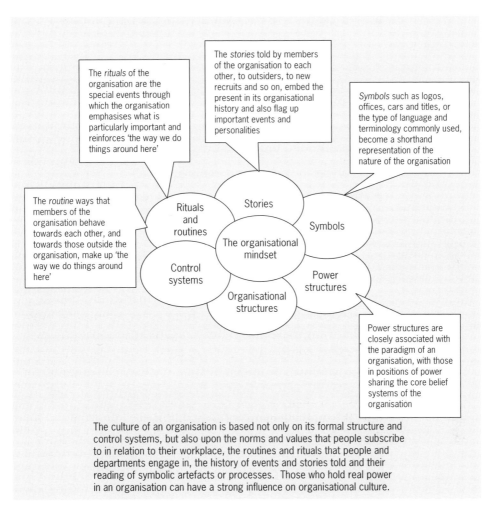

The *rituals* of the organisation are the special events through which the organisation emphasises what is particularly important and reinforces 'the way we do things around here'

The *stories* told by members of the organisation to each other, to outsiders, to new recruits and so on, embed the present in its organisational history and also flag up important events and personalities

Symbols such as logos, offices, cars and titles, or the type of language and terminology commonly used, become a shorthand representation of the nature of the organisation

The *routine* ways that members of the organisation behave towards each other, and towards those outside the organisation, make up 'the way we do things around here'

Rituals and routines

Stories

Symbols

The organisational mindset

Control systems

Power structures

Organisational structures

Power structures are closely associated with the paradigm of an organisation, with those in positions of power sharing the core belief systems of the organisation

The culture of an organisation is based not only on its formal structure and control systems, but also upon the norms and values that people subscribe to in relation to their workplace, the routines and rituals that people and departments engage in, the history of events and stories told and their reading of symbolic artefacts or processes. Those who hold real power in an organisation can have a strong influence on organisational culture.

Figure 1.4 *The cultural web*
            Source: *Adapted from Johnson and Scholes (1999)*

Drivers of change

From the 1970s onwards it is generally true to say that periods of stability, when an organisation's operations could be managed without disruptive change, have become shorter and the necessity to make changes more frequent. Fundamental reasons for this include:

◆ fast and frequent technological change, for example, in manufacturing processes and the displacement of old products with new ones

- globalisation of production of goods and services, markets and competition

- cheaper communication and distribution supported by the revolution in information and communication technology

- government deregulation, including privatisation and legislation to promote competition

- changes in society and demography

- the competition for scarce natural resources

- ecological concerns.

Competitive pressure is an important driver of change. Even if a manufacturing or service sector business has few serious competitors and is under little market pressure to change, there is often pressure from governments and other regulatory agencies. Even those organisations that do not have direct competitors (such as government departments or agencies) will be under pressure to change because of, for example, the requirement to maximise value for money.

Henry Ford reputedly proclaimed 'If it ain't broke, don't fix it.' Yet in today's competitive environment this sentiment would suggest complacency. Yes, you may have a very good process, which produces the goods or services that satisfies current needs, but in a highly competitive world how long will that continue to be the case? (Ford also reputedly joked 'You can have any colour you like as long as it's black!' which is about as far removed as possible from today's situation characterised by overwhelming choice for most goods and services.)

All organisations need to look beyond what works well now, because, whatever services or goods they currently provide, you can be sure that somewhere, someone is aiming to emulate them or better them.

Another major source of change, of which you may have personal experience, is mergers, acquisitions and restructuring activity. Organisations are increasingly subject to restructuring often through mergers with others. It is not unusual for employees to experience this directly several times in their working lives.

What does all this mean for you as an individual employee?

If you work in a relatively stable environment, the future may be relatively predictable and your organisation may be able to plan its future by taking a fairly conservative and measured approach; many organisations go through periods of such relative stability. However, it is likely that there will come a time when even these organisations need to rethink the fundamental way in which they do business.

Many organisations may not have the luxury of relatively stable interludes between significant change episodes. If you work in sectors where this is true you are likely to be faced with more frequent periods of transformational change during your career. While we all need to respond to changing circumstances every day, transformational change requires a much greater level of preparedness based on a deeper awareness of the fundamentals of change, the ability to run with the consequences of change and the need to develop those attributes of skills and competence that will enable you to lead and thrive during periods of change.

Whatever type of organisation you work in, the key to successfully engaging with change is to acquire a clear understanding of the changing organisational context. We will look next at the changing contextual factors that organisations may need to respond to.

The changing organisational context

In the main, successful individuals and organisations are those that are keenly aware of their context – and, in particular, alert to changes in that context. Figure 1.5 visualises the organisational context as a series of concentric circles.

Starting with you and your immediate working environment at the core, you can see how each successive zone denotes a set of influences that become ever more remote from

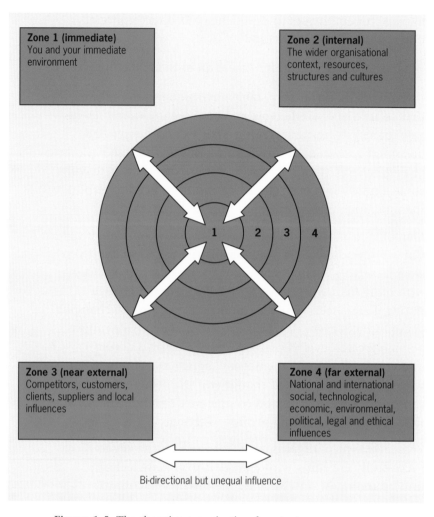

Zone 1 (immediate)
You and your immediate environment

Zone 2 (internal)
The wider organisational context, resources, structures and cultures

Zone 3 (near external)
Competitors, customers, clients, suppliers and local influences

Zone 4 (far external)
National and international social, technological, economic, environmental, political, legal and ethical influences

Bi-directional but unequal influence

Figure 1.5 *The changing organisational context*
Source: *Adapted from Bronfenbrenner (1979)*

you and your immediate working environment, Zone 1. So, Zone 2 refers to the internal structure and resources of the organisation, that is other departments, management structure, human, physical and financial resources; Zone 3 refers to the 'near' external environment, including customers/clients, suppliers and local factors; while Zone 4 refers to the 'far' external environment consisting of social trends, the national and international economic climate, national government policy, the global marketplace, technological innovation and environmental and ethical factors. The bidirectional arrows indicate that influence flows both ways, though not in equal measure.

In the next chapter we will introduce some tools and techniques of strategic analysis to help you understand your organisational context. You will learn to analyse how the forces for change identified in Zones 2–4 could affect you and your working environment. Having gained this understanding of the organisational context you will be in a much better position to develop, plan and engage with change in a way that improves the way you work and adds real value to your organisation.

Activity 1.1
Causes and consequences of change

Aim of this activity

◆ To initiate reflection and discussion on the causes and consequences of change at work.

Useful resources for this activity

◆ *Change, Strategy and Projects at Work*

◆ Resources at work

◆ Discussions with colleagues.

In *Change, Strategy and Projects at Work* we state that organisations are forced into making radical changes for a variety of reasons and mention increased competition and technological advances as examples. For this activity, we want you to think about examples of work-related change from your own experience, decide what you think caused the change and assess the impact of the change on the organisation and the individuals working within it. Use the headings provided below to help you structure your thoughts.

As well as reading the relevant sections in *Change, Strategy and Projects at Work*, look for resources from your workplace such as annual reports, newsletters, organisational objectives, intranets, etc. Finally, don't forget to discuss this with colleagues if possible; they can be a valuable source of 'organisational memory'.

- ◆ Description of change(s)
- ◆ What triggered the change(s)?
- ◆ Impact on the organisation?
- ◆ Impact on individuals?

Activity 1.2
Types of change

Aims of this activity

- ◆ To help you to distinguish between different types of change
- ◆ To help you identify appropriate responses to different types of change.

Useful resources for this activity

- ◆ *Change, Strategy and Projects at Work*
- ◆ Resources at work
- ◆ Discussions with colleagues.

Types of change

On page 9 of *Change, Strategy and Projects at Work* we introduced you to closed, contained and open-ended change.

Think of up to three change events that you know of from your own experience, preferably relating to your current organisation, which fall under each of the three types of change shown in the table below.

Consider how the organisation responded to each type of change, and note your observations in the third column.

Discussion

The real value of this exercise is to get you thinking about different types of change and to understand the point that the 'right' response to change is often not clear-cut because there are often differing views as to why things have happened and what should happen as a result. It is usually only the routine, day-to-day decisions that have definite answers. As soon as you begin to look at the wider challenges facing your organisation, then everything becomes much more complex and subjective – and the scope for disagreement that much greater.

When faced with an important problem that directly affects you, it is all too easy to think that you know the right answer. In the worst situations, people may concentrate on building their own army to support a particular analysis and proposal for action rather than talking with others and really listening to their views. If divergent views are taken into account before a decision is made there is a greater chance that the decision will be a good one and that it will have more widespread support.

Type of event	Description of event	How the organisation responded	Observations
Closed change 1st event 2nd event 3rd event			
Contained change 1st event 2nd event 3rd event			
Open-ended change 1st event 2nd event 3rd event			

2 So what's the strategy?

Introduction

Change which happens by design rather than accident is far more likely to create value and benefits to the organisation. For this to happen, an organisation needs to develop a strategy based on the evidence about what is happening in its context.

You may be thinking that planning at a strategic level is something that you don't do, but perhaps at some time in your personal or working life you may have become dissatisfied with the way things were going, or perhaps some external events may have caused you to take a radical change of direction. In these situations you will very likely have engaged in some personal strategic planning; i.e., taken stock of your current situation, reviewed your goals and thought about how you might achieve them – albeit that this may not have been a particularly conscious or systematic process. Certainly understanding the idea of strategy development will help you understand how and why change is often necessary. Just like individuals, organisations have to take stock, review what their purpose is or could be, determine where they want to be and then plan how to get there. Again the journey metaphor is highly appropriate.

Strategic planning

Organisations can often survive, or even do well, during periods of relative stability, low contextual turbulence and little competition for resources. However, virtually none of these conditions prevail for long in the modern world for any organisation in any sector, public or private. In this chapter we will consider how an organisation's strategic options can be identified by analysing changes in its context.

As well as looking outwards, it will also be necessary for an organisation to look inwards to review its own position, its strengths, weaknesses and available resources, before deciding on the optimum way forward.

Strategic planning can generally be thought of as a three-stage process:

♦ carrying out analyses of the organisation's external context and of its internal conditions and the resources at its disposal

♦ identifying and developing different strategic choices (scenarios) and evaluating their attractiveness to the organisation

♦ implementing the preferred strategy.

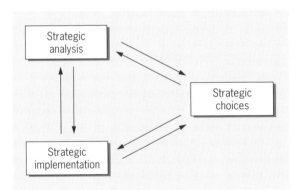

Figure 2.1 *The three stages of strategic planning*
Source: *Adapted from Johnson and Scholes (1999)*

The double arrows in Figure 2.1 indicate the iterative nature of strategic planning. For instance, difficulties in implementing the strategy may result in revisiting the strategic options available; another example could be where an organisation develops its resources but then needs to refer back to a rapidly changing context that has moved on during the intervening period. Under these conditions, the strategy that an organisation adopts may emerge after several iterations. Even then, when undertaking a journey we have to be constantly aware of changes en-route and take appropriate action to ensure that we stay on course for our destination. In a similar way, it would be unrealistic to expect organisational strategy to follow a rigid, linear process.

The intention in this chapter is to give you an overview of a typical approach to the strategic planning process and to introduce you to some of the key concepts and analytical tools commonly used to develop a strategic plan.

Strategic planning addresses four key questions for any organisation:

- Where are we now?
- Where do we want to be?
- How will we get there?
- How can we measure progress and ensure we stay on track to reach our destination?

Table 2.1 presents a typical approach to the strategic planning process and the associated tools and techniques that can be used to try to answer these four key questions. Each of these techniques will be explained in more detail in the following sections of this chapter and in the rest of the book.

Table 2.1 *Strategic planning and implementation process*

Key and subsidiary questions	Inputs/analysis	Outcomes/outputs
Where are we now? What is the purpose of our organisation as expressed in our current mission statement? What are our core values and guiding principles? What are the key factors for success in the sector in which we operate? What expertise do we have? What are we good at doing?	STEEPLE Internal Audit SWOT	An understanding of the impact of external contextual factors facing the organisation An understanding of the internal resources available An understanding of the organisation's strengths and weaknesses in relation to the opportunities and threats facing it A review of the organisation's core values, guiding principles and mission statement

Table 2.1 *(Continued)*

Key and subsidiary questions	Inputs/analysis	Outcomes/outputs
Where do we want to be? Are we still in the same business? Where should the organisation position itself in relation to changes in the external context? Is our mission statement still relevant? If not, what should it be? What is our vision of the desired future state? What are our strategic priorities? What are our strategic objectives?	STEEPLE Internal Audit SWOT Scenario planning What if? analysis Mission statement Vision statement Smart objectives	An exploration of possible futures for the organisation, built on the previous analysis A decision on strategic priorities based on the outcome of this exploration A set of SMART objectives to deliver the strategic priorities A clear and inspiring vision statement that encapsulates the organisation's strategic direction
How will we get there? How do we achieve our strategic objectives? How should the actions be organised? Who will take responsibility for achieving our objectives? What resources will be needed? What are the risk factors that may prevent us from achieving our objectives?	Implementation through projects and project teams Project vision statement, SMART objectives Risk analysis Project budgets and schedules.	A programme defining projects and responsibilities necessary to achieve strategic objectives Lower level targets defined for each project, taking into account identified risk factors Project teams working to achieve required project outcomes
How will we measure progress and stay on track? What are the key milestones? What are the key performance indicators? How often will we review progress? Do we have the necessary skills and unity of purpose to overcome difficulties en-route?	Project milestones for key objectives and deliverables. Project monitoring and review processes. Project team development	Project plans for successful achievement of project level targets

Mission and vision

Mission and vision statements are core concepts of the strategic planning process; however, there is often widespread confusion about the difference between the two – and the distinction is important. A mission statement describes the purpose of the organisation and should answer questions like: 'Why does our organisation exist? What sort of business are we in? What values and guiding principles underpin what we do?'

Mission statement examples – 2008

"Provide society with superior products and services by developing innovations and solutions that improve the quality of life and satisfy customer needs, and to provide employees with meaningful work and advancement opportunities, and investors with a superior rate of return."—Merck

"To enable people and businesses throughout the world to realize their full potential."—Microsoft

"Organize the world's information and make it universally accessible and useful."—Google

A vision statement answers a subtly different question: 'What will future success look like?' A vision statement's purpose is to communicate a credible, appealing and easily understood picture of future success that inspires buy-in. It should extend the expectations, aspirations and motivation of those working to create that future state.

People often feel unsure and cynical about vision statements because the word 'vision' does not follow easily the rational analyses that accompany other aspects of the planning process. This is largely because rational, analytical processes involve 'left-brain' thinking, but the images and imagination suggested by vision calls up right-brain processing. Switching from left to right (or right to left) brain thinking can be disconcerting.

Vision statements often use metaphors to help stretch the imagination and mindset of recipients. Vision statements can articulate the aspirations of an individual or an organisation.

Famous visions from the past

John F Kennedy, 1960:

'By the end of the decade, we will put a man on the moon.'

Martin Luther King, 197:

'I have a dream ....'

Microsoft's 25 year vision statement:

'There will be a personal computer on every desk running Microsoft software.'

Envisioning and visions

Envisioning the future is a well-known tool for improving the likelihood of success. As a rule one doesn't become an Olympic gold medallist by accident. A personal vision of success will help an athlete overcome difficulties and remain committed despite exhausting training schedules. An appropriate personal vision could be to imagine the spectators rising to their feet en masse as the longest jump ever is recorded, or receiving the gold medal on the highest podium.

How a vision is created is less important than its effect and how it is delivered. The ability to inspire other people is an attribute of effective leadership. In the following chapters we will explore how change can be implemented through project working approaches. Matters concerning leadership and vision will resurface there.

Both mission and vision statements should normally be mutually supportive by reflecting, however subtly, an organisation's underlying value system. There could be some mismatch between the current purpose of an organisation and its future vision if one of the aims was to change the organisational culture and the value system underpinning it, though an indication of such change within a modified mission statement could help bring vision and mission into line.

Cautionary note

In order to identify the capabilities, constraints and priorities that the strategic plan for change should address we will examine a number of tools and approaches that are referred to in Table 2.1. This is achieved by conducting external and internal analyses.

It is important to be clear about the nature and purposes of these analyses as well as their limitations. The tools and techniques described below are not new; indeed you may well have come across them in one form or another already. What they aim to do is to help you to simplify, describe and understand a complex reality in a systematic way. By following these approaches an organisation can build up the evidence base on which to make its strategic decisions. What the approaches cannot do is to provide complete certainty that a chosen strategy is the right one.

In order to make sense of a complex social reality, we need to simplify it by identifying those factors that are of most importance to us in a particular context. This is what the tools and techniques that follow enable you to do. In the process of simplification and prioritisation we inevitably make choices that exclude other possibilities. This is why each decision regarding adopted choices must be justified. This is best achieved within a collaborative setting where different perspectives can be aired and a balanced judgement arrived at.

Another important point to bear in mind is that the analytical process is one that requires some deep thinking – superficial thinking will lead to a superficial analysis that in turn is unlikely to produce a sensible or robust strategy. The techniques described below are just tools that need to be used correctly to produce the best possible outcome.

Finally, although we introduce you to the tools and suggest some questions and issues that you may wish to include in your analyses, these suggestions are offered without reference to your own organisation's particular situation and context. It is imperative that when you apply these approaches you do so by comprehensively including data relevant to your organisation's specific context. You will need to decide what questions and issues are most important in this respect.

The external context

Increasingly, a winning strategy will require information about events and conditions outside the organisation. Only with this information can an organisation prepare for new changes and challenges arising from, for example, sudden shifts in the world economy and in the nature and content of knowledge itself.
Drucker (1997)[1] quoted in Paton and McCalman (2000)[2]

In the quotation Drucker is referring to the importance of scanning the external context to gather and then evaluate information which can be used to determine a strategy for change. The first technique considered is a STEEPLE analysis, which is aligned to Zones 3 and 4, the 'near' and 'far' external contexts. (Refer back to Figure 1.5: The changing organisational context.)

STEEPLE analysis – Zones 3 and 4

STEEPLE is an acronym representing the major contextual dimensions to be included in the analysis of the external context. However, there are variations on this acronym as described in the following box.

STEEPLE, PESTLE and PEST

STEEPLE identifies Social, Technological, Economic, Environmental, Political, Legal and Ethical dimensions.

---

[1] Drucker (1997)
[2] Paton and McCalman (2000)

Shorter variations of this acronym are in common use; for example:

PESTLE identifies Political, Economic, Social, Technological, Legal and Environmental dimensions.

PEST identifies only Political, Economic, Social, Technological dimensions.

The shorter acronyms refer to the same analysis, but do not explicitly bring out all those dimensions that should be exposed to active investigation. For this reason we will adopt STEEPLE.

In these acronyms the term 'environmental' is used in its generally familiar sense, rather than referring to an organisation's external 'environment'; example of issues in this dimension are pollution and sustainability.

Figure 2.2 (*external context*) represents an organisation surrounded by and interacting with its external context (Refer back to Figure 1.5: The changing organisational context) through the STEEPLE dimensions.

The external context includes Zones 3 and 4, the near and far external regions of the organisational context, shown in

Figure 2.2 *'The external context'*

Figure 2.3. The factors considered in these zones, particularly
Zone 4, are often broad, sweeping changes, trends and
influences that may be more difficult to relate directly to your
organisation.

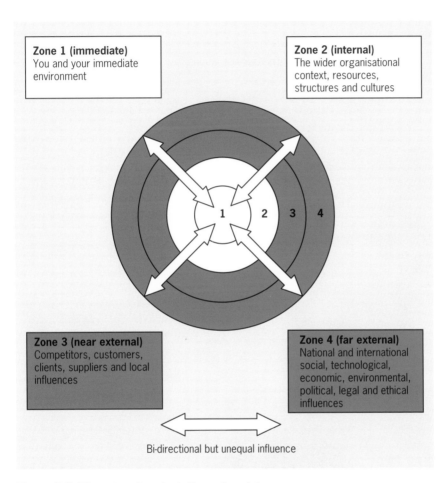

Figure 2.3 *The external context: Zones 3 and 4*

Source: *Adapted from Bronfenbrenner (1979)*

In general, each dimension – social, technological, economic,
environmental, political, legal and ethical – of the external
context in which an organisation functions should be explored
in turn. The aim is to actively identify the relevant external
drivers for change within each dimension and to try to predict
the possible consequences for the organisation over both the
short and longer term. We will use Table 2.2 to achieve this next.

Table 2.2 *STEEPLE Analysis – dimensions and drivers*

Dimensions	Zone 3 – Potential drivers in the 'near' context	Zone 4 – Potential drivers in the 'far' context
Social – What are the main social, demographic and cultural aspects to consider now and in the next 3–5 years?	Availability of appropriately qualified and experienced workforce Social and cultural role and reputation of the organisation in the locality Who are our key stakeholders and what is the nature of our relationship with them?	Social attitudes and behaviours General lifestyle changes Changes in distribution and demographics of populations Impact of different mixes of culture
Technological – What are the current technological imperatives, changes and innovations to consider now and in the next 3–5 years?	What technologies are 'state of the art' in our sector? Are we at the cutting edge? Are the latest technologies available to us locally?	What are the major current and emerging technologies of relevance to my organisation? What are the costs and benefits of investing in them?
Economic – What are the important economic factors to consider now and in the next 3–5 years?	What is our performance in key markets/sectors? How do we compare to other organisations in our sector? Are our income streams reliable and stable? Do we have good relationships with customers, clients, suppliers and funders? Do we make a significant contribution to the local economy?	What is the impact of economic globalisation on our organisation? What are the key global economic trends that have, or are likely to have, an impact on our organisation?
Environmental – What are the environmental considerations locally and globally now and in the next 3–5 years?	What is the local environmental impact of our operations? How does the state of the local environment impact on our operations? How does our environmental strategy and impact compare with other similar organisations in our sector? Will environmental considerations affect the sustainability of our operations in the future?	What are the national and international environmental impacts on our operations? What kind of statements or claims about our environmental strategy do we make to the world? Are these claims justified by our actions?

Table 2.2 *(Continued)*

Dimensions	Zone 3 – Potential drivers in the 'near' context	Zone 4 – Potential drivers in the 'far' context
Political – What are the key political drivers of relevance now and in the next 3–5 years?	How do local political institutions, policies and affiliations impact on our operations?	How do national and international political institutions, policies and affiliations impact on our operations?
Legal – What current and impending national and international legislation and regulations affect my organisation/sector now and in the next 3–5 years?	Disability legislation? Data protection legislation? Health and safety legislation? Environmental legislation? Anti-discrimination legislation? Tax legislation? Wage legislation?	The impact of legislation in other national jurisdictions The impact of international treaties and agreements, e.g. on human rights or climate change
Ethical – What are the key ethical considerations?	Are there external professional codes of practice/ethical codes that apply to the organisation?	What kinds of ethical statements/claims does the organisation make to the world? Are these claims justified by what we actually do?

Table 2.2 provides an indication of the drivers that are likely to relate to each of the STEEPLE dimensions for the near and far external contexts, though you should not take these as definitive and exhaustive. Also, not all the dimensions or drivers will have equal significance for any particular organisation, so it is important to seek to identify those that are likely to have most significance for you and your organisation. For instance, a local government organisation is likely to be less affected by economic globalisation in the economic dimension when compared with a manufacturing business, though it is likely to be more strongly affected by changes in local policy in the political dimension. Also some overlap between dimensions are likely to arise; for example, political and legal contexts, because politicians are primarily responsible for introducing legislation. However, don't automatically reject any of the dimensions out of hand. Because the significance of dimensions and drivers

can change with time, it is important that prior assumptions should not be fed into a STEEPLE analysis. One of the benefits of a STEEPLE analysis is that it may direct you to think about issues that you would not normally consider as being important. Therefore, it's best to take a 'blank canvas' approach initially and consider anew the possible relevance of all dimensions and drivers, selecting out those for further examination that are considered to have the greatest change significance for your organisation.

A STEEPLE analysis should, ideally, be carried out in a brainstorming, collaborative environment. Having identified those dimensions and drivers that have relevance to the organisation the next step is to identify the dimensions and drivers that are likely to significantly affect the sector in which the organisation operates now as well as sectors into which it may venture in the future. To get the most out of the process it is necessary to frame questions in relation to each dimension and each potential driver. Refer to the example provided in the box that follows.

Example of review approach – Social dimension – far external context

Question: What issues, in the wider world (Zone 4), that relate to social attitudes and behaviours are significant in the organisation's operating sector?

Possible response: Increased social interaction using social networking sites lead to wider customer networking and critiquing in relation to commercial products or services.

The driver identified in this case is the development of on-line social networking.

Subsequent questions could be framed to elicit how this is likely to particularly affect customer satisfaction ratings for the products of the organisation.

A further question could pick up on the demographic profiles of those most likely to engage with social networking and whether this could influence sales to different customer age groups.

Questioning should continue until the line of enquiry is exhausted.

Carrying through a STEEPLE analysis in relation to the far external context will support systematic thinking about the 'bigger picture' when it is all too easy to focus only on issues that are inside the organisation or within its immediate context. As the global situation become more volatile and change happens more rapidly, organisations need to frequently, or even continually, scan the context in which they operate for indications of potential change.

As the analysis so far has been focused on the far external environment the cycle needs to be repeated to elicit those issues, factors and drivers that relate to the near external context too (Zone 3 in Figure 2.3). By 'near' we don't just mean closer geographically, but also closer to the organisation in terms of interactions and influences. Examples of factors to focus on in this part of the analysis could include things such as changes in your customer/ client base, supply chain issues, external funding changes, relationships with key external stakeholders, changes in the market structure, specific new technologies, labour supply, skills shortages and so forth. There may also be some geographically 'near' factors that you wish to consider in this analysis; indeed, some of the factors just mentioned may fall into that category. Examples of geographically near factors to consider could be things like local transport infrastructure or local planning laws. One effect of globalisation is to blur the distinction between global and local as local events and perceptions can so easily impact on the global scene and vice versa.

> **Example of review approach – Economic dimension – near external context**
>
> If one of your organisation's major suppliers or distributors decided to introduce and develop 'lean manufacturing' processes how could this affect your own organisation's working practices and, possibly, also your own internal organisational culture? How might this impact upon the way business is carried out between the two organisations within the same supply chain?

The analysis described so far has not included an indication of the time frames over which influences from the changing context should be projected. Questions to be asked could include 'What does this mean for our organisation over the short term (perhaps 1–2 years) or the longer term (perhaps 3–5 years)?' The agreed responses to these lines of enquiry will of course be important for determining strategic options for change over the corresponding time frames. Remember that some drivers of change can grow in significance over a period of time whilst others can create abrupt and potentially disruptive change.

Engaging fully with a STEEPLE analysis should result in an in-depth understanding of how changes in the near and far external contexts might impact on the current and future plans of your organisation. You should remember that there can be no absolute certainty in the outcomes of such analyses, but after having carried out such analyses, you should certainly be in a better position to develop a more robust strategy for dealing with change in whatever form it presents.

The success of the approach will depend crucially on the thoroughness of the research undertaken to identify those drivers in the external (near or far) context that have the potential to impact on the organisation and its mission. Again, the best outcomes will result when this analysis has been undertaken in a collaborative setting where a sufficient breadth of perception and expertise is available to ensure that the analysis is comprehensively critiqued.

One potential drawback of a STEEPLE analysis is that it can become too focused on the historical or current context. When using this framework for analysis, although you should begin with reference to the present, then develop your line of enquiry towards what you think the organisation's external context will look like in the future. You should remember that each dimension is dynamic and that your STEEPLE analysis represents a snapshot taken at a particular time. Ideally, your organisation will repeat this analysis on a regular basis to keep abreast of new developments that are likely to have an impact on its strategic plans.

Summary – STEEPLE process

In carrying out a STEEPLE analysis it is necessary to go through two passes of the process:

Pass 1: Significant drivers in the far external context (Zone 4 in Figure 2.3)

Pass 2: Significant drivers in the near external context (Zone 3 in Figure 2.3)

Identify issues and consequences for your organisation starting with the current situation, then extending consideration to the short term (e.g., 1–2 years) and the longer term (e.g., 3–5 years). The time frame of concern is likely to vary considerably depending upon operating sector. (Five years is a long time in some sectors, e.g., computing or ICTs.)

This would be a good time to work through Activity 2.1

The internal and immediate contexts

In this section we will review aspects of Zones 1 and 2 of the organisational context – the internal organisational context and the immediate organisational context. These analyses are necessary to identify key issues that the individual and the organisation may need to address to thrive in a changing world. It requires a dispassionate appraisal of the strengths and weaknesses of both the organisation and the individual – as well as the resources available for effective performance.

The internal organisational context – Zone 2

Figure 2.4 identifies Zone 2. An internal review is necessary to identify those resources issues and structures that:

◆ may constrain or enhance the future direction of the organisation and thus influence the choice of change strategy

◆ will determine, in broad terms, the feasibility of introducing the necessary changes through the various projects that a change programme may initiate.

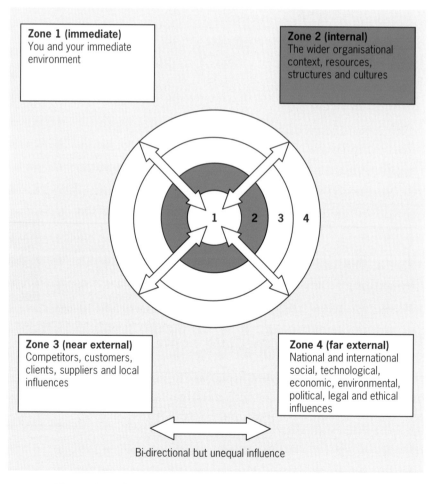

Figure 2.4 *The internal context: Zone 2*

Source: *Adapted from Bronfenbrenner (1979)*

These requirements are to ensure that any change proposal is broadly grounded in what is feasible. However, the detailed planning of resources for any projects that cascade downwards as a change strategy is implemented will be undertaken on a project-by-project basis at a later stage.

In carrying out an internal analysis it is necessary to be clear about its scope – what will be covered and what won't. For example, is the area of proposed change focused on a fairly narrow operational matter relating to a particular department, or do the issues cut across several departments? The areas to be investigated and the amount of detail will be driven by the need to produce sound recommendations. The resource categories that need to be investigated are depicted in Table 2.3, but the focus of resource investigation will be

Table 2.3 *The internal organisational context*[3]

Resource type	Typical Queries
Physical resources	What is the age and condition of the plant, equipment, buildings and so on? Do these physical resources extend or constrain the organisation's effectiveness with regard to the proposed change area?
Human resources	What skills and competencies currently exist and how are these dispersed amongst the workforce and/or departments? What technological competencies does the organisation possess? How adaptable and innovative is the workforce? Are there plentiful opportunities for learning and development? How is the organisation structured currently? Will the organisational structure help or hinder organisational effectiveness going forward?
Financial resources	Is the organisation on a sound financial footing? Is the organisation capable of attracting further investment if required? Are financial resources deployed effectively and efficiently? Are budgets devolved to the appropriate level to aid innovation?
Intangibles	Is the culture of the organisation open to new ideas and innovation? Does the workforce feel valued and rewarded? Does the organisation project a positive image to the outside world through its marketing and communications activities?

Source: *Adapted from Johnson and Scholes (1999)*

---

[3] Johnson and Scholes (1999)

guided by those key factors that are critical to success in your organisation's sector of operation.

Although it is important not to spend time investigating resource areas that lie outside the agreed terms of reference, if the scope appears too narrow to address the underlying problems, then the scope could be widened to ensure that the problem areas are fully covered. For instance, there could be merit in considering the transfer of a resource from one area which is over-resourced to one which it was felt would be under-resourced, in order that the proposed change could be supported.

The resources identified in Table 2.3 include both the hard (financial and physical) resources as well as the soft resources, those associated with people, their attitudes, intellect and so on. Soft resources are considerably more difficult to appraise accurately as well as manage. At the start of this book we considered how an individual faced with change can react in a way characterised by the coping cycle. As you read earlier in the box headed *Readiness to change – culture, power and politics*, the culture associated with groups within an organisation and of the whole organisation can present a significant constraint and resistance to change.

The information obtained by conducting a resource audit can be used to suggest:

♦ realistic objectives that need to be set in the area of the proposed change

♦ how those objectives might be achieved: for example, the willingness and adaptability of the workforce in developing new skills could be critical factors when introducing challenging new technology into a key process area.

This would be a good time to work through Activity 2.2

The immediate context – Zone 1

Finally, in this section on scanning the organisational context we look at Zone 1 (the immediate context in Figure 2.5), where the focus is on you and your immediate working environment.

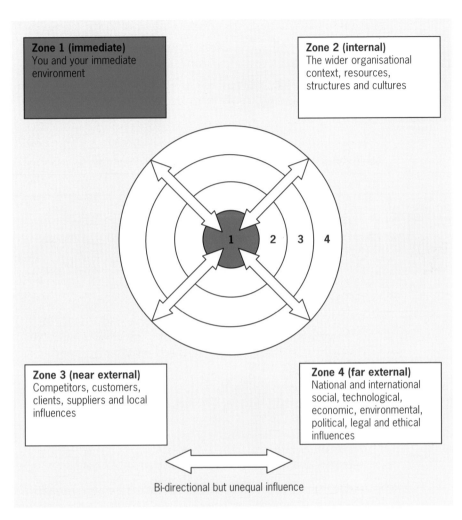

Zone 1 (immediate)
You and your immediate environment

Zone 2 (internal)
The wider organisational context, resources, structures and cultures

Zone 3 (near external)
Competitors, customers, clients, suppliers and local influences

Zone 4 (far external)
National and international social, technological, economic, environmental, political, legal and ethical influences

Bi-directional but unequal influence

Figure 2.5 *The internal context: Zone 1*
Source: *Adapted from Bronfenbrenner (1979)*

Again, there is an aspect of 'taking stock' – looking at your current position – but with a definite forward-looking perspective. Having scanned the external contexts and the internal context you need to bear the results of your previous analyses in mind as you seek to understand how change may affect you and your work role in the future or, conversely, to see if you can suggest any changes that you might actively pursue to improve your own position and add value to your organisation.

This would be a good time to work through Activity 2.3

Use Table 2.4 as a basis for conducting your Zone 1 scan. Remember, though, that this is purely an indicative example of the sort of areas you may want to look at and the kind of questions you may want to ask – don't hesitate to alter the format or contents to make it more relevant to you in your specific context.

Table 2.4 *You and your immediate working environment*

Aspect	Possible questions
Values/ethics/culture	What personal values underpin your practice? Are you operating under a formal ethical code/code of conduct? Are there, or can you foresee, any conflicts and/or contradictions between your work and your values/ethical code? What is the culture of your immediate working environment? Does it align well with your personal values and any ethical code/code of conduct that pertains in your workplace?
Relationships	What are your key working relationships with colleagues within your immediate working environment and in the wider organisation? Will you need to forge new relationships to help you to perform more effectively in the future?
Knowledge, skills and personal attributes	Can you list the knowledge, skills and other personal attributes required to perform your duties effectively now? Can you identify any knowledge, skills and personal attributes that you will need to develop in the short to medium term? What are your personal ambitions and aspirations? Are there clear development opportunities available to you?
Infrastructure	Do you have access to adequate communications and administrative systems to allow you to perform your role effectively now and in the short to medium term?
Suggestions for improvement	Can you identify changes that would improve your personal effectiveness and performance and/or add value to your organisation?

The information from the external and internal analyses described so far can now be brought together and used for an assessment of the overall situation carried out through a SWOT analysis.

Assessing the overall picture – SWOT Analysis

A Strengths, Weaknesses, Opportunities and Threats (SWOT) analysis will normally be conducted within a team setting to achieve a consensus outcome. Figure 2.6 indicates the matrix used to structure the analysis.

	Strengths • • • •	Weaknesses • • • •
Opportunities • • • •	[How do I use these strengths to take advantage of these opportunities?]	[How do I overcome the weaknesses that prevent me taking advantage of these opportunities?]
Threats • • • •	[How do I use these strengths to reduce the likelihood and impact of these threats?]	[How do I address the weaknesses that will make these threats a reality?]

Figure 2.6 *SWOT matrix*

Source: *Reproduced from JISC PM Infokit*

You should be able to see how the previous analyses feed in to the SWOT analysis. In particular, STEEPLE provides an indication of where the opportunities and threats may arise (see Figure 2.7), whilst the internal analyses should help you to understand personal and organisational strengths and weaknesses.

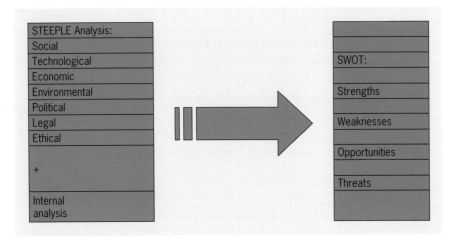

Figure 2.7 *STEEPLE to SWOT*

The analysis starts by focusing first on the strengths of the organisation (or department or group, if the change situation requires this). Examples of strengths could be, for example, the technical expertise residing in the research and development department or the current financial reserves. A list of strengths is agreed and entered into the Strengths cell. The process is then repeated to identify and enter bullets into the three other cells: Weaknesses, Opportunities and then Threats. Examples of a weakness could be that an existing product range did not provide all the features or ease of use that customers indicate are important to them.

Filling in the top row of the SWOT matrix (Strengths and Weaknesses) provides a view of the organisation's current position; that is, an answer to the question 'Where are we now?'

Entering bullets in the Opportunities and Threats areas indicates answers to the following questions:

◆ What opportunities arise from the changes or anticipated changes in the environment that the organisation would be well placed to exploit as a result of its strengths?

◆ What threats could the organisation be exposed to as a result of its weaknesses?

For example, if you identified an upsurge in consumer/client demand for a new product or service you could say that this represents an opportunity to increase your market share, as well as help more clients.

The next step would be to examine your organisation's strengths and weaknesses in relation to the opportunity identified. For example, you may have the skills needed to produce a particular product or service (strength), but perhaps you don't have the capacity (weakness). You would then need to consider ways of increasing your organisation's capacity to meet the potential increase in demand.

The outcome of the SWOT analysis should be a series of statements indicating what opportunities the organisation might successfully pursue as a result of its strengths and any actions that should be taken to eliminate or reduce its exposure to threats.

As you go through a SWOT analysis, you may find that there is quite a lot of overlap between the four quadrants; for example, opportunities can also be seen as threats and often there is a weakness to set against a strength. You should not worry about this. Just remember that the SWOT analysis is a way of organising your thoughts about the potential for change. Remember too that the tools we describe are not infallible, but, as a way of structuring individual and group thought processes, they should help you to reach rational conclusions before deciding on the course of action needed. The quality of the outcomes will be determined by the effort that is put into researching the basis on which observations are made and the time and energy allotted to the task of critically reviewing all propositions.

> **This would be a good time to work through Activity 2.4**

Having conducted the STEEPLE, internal analyses and SWOT, the organisation should be in a better position to understand what options are possible to change the way it carries out its business in the future. However, there is no guarantee of certainty in how the external and internal contexts will develop, so in the run-up to making an informed strategic choice for implementing change, more questions should be asked. Refer to the box headed *What if? – scenario planning.*

What if...? – Scenario planning

Scenario planning is an approach used in some organisations to support the development of strategies that are robust and flexible. The method, originating in military planning circles, assumes that a STEEPLE analysis of the external environment (or a close equivalent) has been carried out. This is to identify the most likely drivers of change, usually in the longer term (for example, 5–10 years).

Next a range of scenarios is created based on selected drivers of change. These are usually distilled down to about three plausible ones which include some contentious or uncomfortable elements that serve to bring out hidden weaknesses or inflexibility in an organisation's potential response. Brainstorming of the issues associated with each of the scenarios is carried out by up to about ten participants. The selected outputs of the brainstorming sessions can then be fed into the strategic options decision-making process.

This approach is helpful for longer-term planning where assumptions based on current trends are less easily extrapolated. Participants are encouraged to think creatively about the assumptions adopted, the various responses on the part of the organisation and the outcomes likely to follow.

Change proposals and strategic choice

Decisions on the optimal way forward will naturally vary depending upon context; however, in general, Johnson and Scholes (1999)[4] suggest three major criteria, against which the appropriateness of all change proposals should be evaluated (Figure 2.8):

- ◆ Suitability – do the proposals address the circumstances in which the organisation is operating or is expecting to operate?

- ◆ Acceptability – do the proposals offer a good return on the investment needed and present an acceptable level of risk and will stakeholders in the organisation react favourably?

- ◆ Feasibility – can the proposed outcomes of the change programme actually be achieved? Are the necessary resources and capabilities available?

---

[4]Johnson and Scholes (1999)

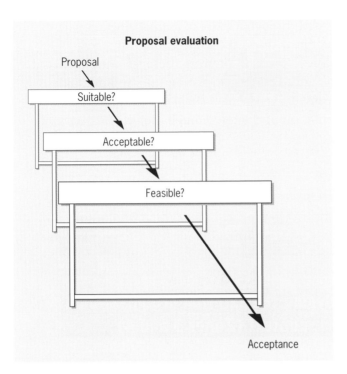

Figure 2.8 *Evaluation hurdles*

The analyses described in this section provide the means to establish an appropriate strategy for change. The scale and significance of the proposals of a change programme may vary considerably. On the one hand the changes needed may be relatively modest and align with the existing organisational strategy. On the other hand a radical transformation may be required and will be framed within a radically reshaped strategy.

Whatever the scale of change proposed, a key requirement is that it is communicated to all the stakeholders to gain widespread buy-in. A vision statement is an important component of this requirement, but it is the organisation's strategic plan which sets out the key priorities and objectives that provides the detailed route map of how to make that vision a reality. Often the strategic plan is

This would be a good time to work through Activity 2.5

implemented through a series of annual 'operational plans' that break down the strategic objectives into 'programmes', 'projects' or 'work packages' with dedicated resources, agreed performance indicators and clear lines of responsibility. In the next chapter we explore the implementation of change through project working.

Activity 2.1
Analysing the external organisational context (Zones 3 and 4)

Aims of this activity

◆ To help you prepare an analysis of the current external context in which your organisation operates

◆ To help you prepare an analysis of what you think the external context will look like in 5 years

◆ To compile a list of what needs to change if your organisation is to be successful in this new context.

Useful resources for this activity

◆ *Change, Strategy and Projects at Work*

◆ Resources at work

◆ Discussions with colleagues

◆ Media sources

◆ STEEPLE analysis template.

STEEPLE Analysis

The first column of the following STEEPLE template contains some prompts to start you thinking about the type of contextual factors you might consider as you complete the STEEPLE analysis for your organisation. Examples of possible drivers are given in Table 2.2 on page 30 of *Change, Strategy and Projects at Work*. This isn't meant to be an exhaustive list and you should feel free to include any other questions you think are relevant to your own organisation based on your understanding of the current context. Try to make this as specific to your organisation as possible. For example, if rapid developments in information and communication technologies are affecting your organisation, think about the areas in which they have most impact. Is it in the delivery of the service to customers/clients, reducing your cost base or developing new products and services? Note down these areas/impacts in column three.

Having completed your analysis of the current context, in the fourth column set out what you think the main contextual factors will be in the next 5 years. Think about how they will influence what you do and the way you produce or provide products and services. For example, think about how demand might be affected and how your suppliers and funding may change. Remember you need to consider both the near and far external context in your analyses, so you may want to use separate STEEPLE templates for each aspect initially.

Finally, think about the changes your organisation needs to make to be successful in this new context. You'll find some questions to prompt your thinking at the end of the table.

Activity 2.1 STEEPLE analysis template

STEEPLE dimensions	Current contextual drivers (0–2 years)	How might they affect the organisation?	Future contextual drivers (3–5 years)	How might they affect the organisation?
Social – What are the main social, demographic and cultural aspects to consider now and in the next 3–5 years?				
Technological – What are the current technological imperatives, changes and innovations to consider now and in the next 3–5 years?				
Economic – What are the important economic factors to consider now and in the next 3–5 years?				

Environmental – What are the environmental considerations locally and globally now and in the next 3–5 years?			
Political – What are the key political drivers of relevance now and in the next 3–5 years?			
Legislative – What current and impending national and international legislation and regulations affect my organisation/sector now and in the next 3–5 years?			
Ethical – What are the key ethical considerations?			

Activity 2.1

The prospects for your organisation – how far it will need to change:

- ◆ Is your organisation facing radical changes?
- ◆ What are the key trends/factors/challenges likely to affect your organisation in the future?
- ◆ Are there clear opportunities and threats posed by these trends/factors/challenges?
- ◆ Are there clear actions your organisation can take in response to these factors?

Discussion

As organisations work to improve the fundamentals of their business, they need to be aware that those fundamentals may be undergoing rapid change and the nature of the business itself may be transformed. For example, as the introduction of personal computers decimated the market for mainframe computers, so commentators now regularly speculate about what will replace the PC. You could use your work on this activity as a basis for discussion with colleagues in your organisation. What do your colleagues think? How far is there agreement as to what major environmental change may impact upon your organisation over the next 5 years? Your STEEPLE analysis will undoubtedly be much stronger, and you will have more confidence in the results, if you are able to take into account different perspectives.

Thinking about the external trends and challenges that face your organisation in the external context now and in the future should have given you some ideas about what needs to change. These ideas will help you to begin to focus in on ideas for a specific change/improvement project proposal that you will develop later using the knowledge and skills gained in subsequent chapters of this book. This kind of contextual scan is an important analytical tool that will provide you with a framework for understanding what needs to change and how change could be implemented.

Activity 2.2
Internal organisational analysis (Zone 2)

Aims of this activity

- To assess the strength of the key resources that your organisation has to exploit opportunities and counter threats.

Useful resources for this activity

- *Change, Strategy and Projects at Work*
- Resources at work
- Discussions with colleagues.

Key resources – strengths and weaknesses

The following template will help you to assess the strengths and weaknesses of your organisation's position in relation to the opportunities and threats in the external context by taking into account the resources that your organisation has to exploit or counter them. Bear in mind that you may have identified resource factors other than the ones mentioned in Table 2.3 on page 37 of *Change, Strategy and Projects at Work* and it is fine to include them in this activity. The idea is for you to produce something that corresponds to your real work situation rather than forcing you to make your work situation fit in with the text.

Activity 2.2 Internal organisational analysis

Resource category	Strengths	Weaknesses
Physical resources		
Human resources		
Financial resources		
Intangibles		

Activity 2.3
You and your immediate work context (Zone 1)

Aims of this activity

◆ To assess the strengths and weaknesses of you position in your immediate work context and to identify actions you can take to reinforce strengths and overcome weaknesses.

Useful resources for this activity

◆ *Change, Strategy and Projects at Work*

◆ Resources at work

◆ Discussions with colleagues.

Using Table 2.4 on page 40 of *Change, Strategy and Projects at Work* as a prompt identify and list the strengths and weaknesses that exist in your immediate work context. Think about actions you could take to reinforce the strengths, overcome the weaknesses and then list them in column 4.

Activity 2.3 You and your immediate work context

Aspect	Strengths	Weaknesses	Actions
Values/ethics/ culture			
Relationships			

Knowledge, skills and personal attributes			
Infrastructure			

Activity 2.4
SWOT Analysis

Aim of this activity

◆ To help you to complete a SWOT analysis for your organisation.

Useful resources for this activity:

◆ *Change, Strategy and Projects at Work*

◆ Resources at work

◆ Discussions with colleagues

Refer to the explanations of the external and internal analyses and use the outcomes from the external and internal analyses of your own workplace context (Activities 2.1, 2.2 and 2.3) to complete a SWOT analysis for your organisation using the example below as a guide. A blank template is included below for your use/adaptation.

Example SWOT analysis

Organisational SWOT Analysis		
	Strengths Technical skills Low cost base Well respected brand	**Weaknesses** Poor management skills Lack of investment in training Poor ICT infrastructure
Opportunities Expanding home market E-commerce New technology coming on stream	[Can I use these strengths to take advantage of these opportunities?]	[Can I overcome the weaknesses that prevent me taking advantage of these opportunities?]
Threats New competition Low staff morale Old product range	[Can I use these strengths to reduce the likelihood and impact of these threats?]	[Can I address the weaknesses that will make these threats a reality?]

SWOT template

Organisational SWOT Analysis		
	Strengths	Weaknesses
Opportunities		
Threats		

Adapted from the JISC SWOT template (online) accessed on 17 March 2006 at http://www.jiscinfonet.ac.uk/InfoKits/project-management/pestle-swot

Discussion

Having completed the initial organisational SWOT on your own in the first instance, show it to a few colleagues and get their views. It is a good idea for SWOTs to be a collective effort rather than just the work of one individual. Everyone will come up with different factors that they consider to be strengths, weaknesses, opportunities and threats. Of course, if there is a consensus about particular factors, maybe those are the ones that should be selected as a priority for further examination. Make a note of any patterns or trends you see emerging and modify your initial SWOT as you see fit.

Activity 2.5
Trends and futures

Aims of this activity

◆ To research trends within your organisation's sector

◆ To anticipate possible futures.

Useful resources for this activity

◆ *Change, Strategy and Projects at Work*

◆ Resources at work

◆ Discussions with colleagues

◆ Media sources.

Future change

Consider the results of all your previous analyses and any other relevant sources you have to hand, or can access easily, to forecast what your organisation's operating context may look like in

5 years time. Obtaining the views of people you work with, including colleagues, customers/clients and suppliers would undoubtedly help you to develop your thinking.

In the table below, first fill in the current objectives and priorities of your organisation. Next, fill in what you think the organisation's objectives and priorities will be looking forward five years and speculate, if you can, about what might happen after that.

Activity 2.5 Forecast shift of organisation's objectives

Period	Organisational objectives
Current	
In 5 years	
Beyond 5 years	

Discussion

Organisations need to anticipate change and think creatively. They need to create a vision of the future and actively pursue it. The only alternative is to be like a small boat tossed around on the sea as we repeatedly react to the latest external event. Hopefully, completing this activity has helped you to do some reading and creative thinking about where your organisation is going and how its priorities will change in the future. Other people within your organisation may have different ideas, but that is fine because it is through debate that better-quality decisions will emerge.

The extent to which you were able to meet the objectives of this activity clearly depends on your existing knowledge of the sector and the research sources available to you. However, the value of undertaking the activity lies in the process of thinking about where your organisation is heading and the issues it could face in the future. Researching trends, seeking to anticipate change, thinking creatively about possible futures and taking an active rather than a reactive approach are all vital skills and attitudes that you will need to develop.

Implementing change through project working

Introduction

In the previous chapters we have discussed the nature of change and introduced you to tools and techniques to help you analyse the changing context within which you and your organisation operate. In this chapter we begin to show you how you can use project working tools and techniques to implement change in the workplace in a systematic and effective way.

You will learn more about project working in the next chapter, but the definition of a project that we use in this book is:

A project is a temporary endeavour involving a connected sequence of activities and a range of resources, which is designed to achieve a specific and unique outcome, which operates within time, cost and quality constraints and which is often used to introduce change. (Lake 1997)[1].

Projects are increasingly the way in which strategic objectives are achieved because in an era of rapid change, organisations are forced to review strategic objectives more frequently and strive to achieve them more quickly. The scope for continuing routine operations and tasks in organisations has tended to diminish over time and there is no sign of this trend changing. Nowadays, organisations in all sectors have to adapt to changes of such rapidity and diversity that many work roles now incorporate characteristics of project working (even if it is not explicitly recognised as such) to a far greater extent than ever before. Yet, as with change and strategic planning, knowledge about the principles of project working is still

---

[1] Lake (1997)

too often the preserve of 'experts' – project managers – who may or may not have had some formal training in a project management methodology. Once again, it is our contention that an awareness and understanding of project working tools and techniques should be much more widely spread within the workforce of a modern organisation than is currently the case.

What is a project?

Looking again at Lake's definition and extracting the key features that are common to all projects:

- A project is a temporary endeavour because it should have a clearly defined and agreed start and finish date.

- A project involves a connected sequence of activities: however short and localised, or long and complex, a project will have a specific set of activities that are linked together and which must be completed to achieve a successful outcome.

- Each project's aims and objectives will be unique to that project, though some of the activities (or even all) may have been carried out previously in a different project or work situation.

- A project requires a range of resources: all projects should have a quantifiable resource requirement, for example, people, systems, space, time, or specialist input.

- A project will have a specific and unique outcome in that the exact work or sequence of work will not have been carried out previously in the same organisation: the success of the outcome will be evaluated in terms of the specification of what the project was expected to achieve as well as the time taken and the final cost of achieving the required outcome.

- A project is often used as an instrument for change. One or more projects may be instigated to support a strategic change programme. In these cases, carrying through projects can have significant implications in terms of differences in the way people are expected to work, communicate or go about their daily lives.

Projects can cover many different types of activity. For example, they can investigate a specific problem, research a new product or service, or be set up to implement the findings of an earlier project. They can be carried out entirely in-house by an organisation's own staff, make use of external consultants, involve several organisations working together in a consortium, or any mix of these.

The durations and budgets of projects can vary enormously. A project to re-equip a single office may take 2 weeks and have a budget of perhaps £1000 or less, whilst a project to host the Olympic Games may cost many billions of pounds and take several years. Hosting the Olympic Games provides regular, interesting case studies where significant opportunities for change for the host nation become possible through a cascade of projects needed to support the event itself, but with longer lasting implications for the host nation. For example, upgrading the transport infrastructure of the region in which the games will be held or changing public attitudes towards health and fitness.

From the definition of a project, it should be clear that all projects will share some common features; for example, all projects may be evaluated against the three generic criteria of time, cost and quality and all projects will follow a similar life cycle. However, there will be differences in the way that projects are organised and implemented dependent upon the context in which a project is carried out. See the box *Project methodologies*.

The ideas presented in following sections are broadly applicable to a wide range of projects that vary in size, complexity, cost and timescale.

Project methodologies

A project methodology can be defined as a set of guidelines or principles relating to a process for accomplishing a successful project outcome. You may find many alternative definitions, but this one suits our purpose.

Different operating sectors are likely to adopt different project methodologies. For example a project in manufacturing industry is likely to be organised in a way that is suited to the context of manufacturing industry and use project processes that are suited to that context; on the other hand, a project carried out in an academic environment such as a college or university may adopt a different project methodology more suited to the very different context in which the project is implemented.

Some methodologies will have been specifically developed by individual organisations for use in their specialist fields, whilst others may be adopted in some sectors as the de facto standards.

As an example, an organisation carrying out a project for a government department in the United Kingdom will be expected to adopt a project methodology based on PRINCE (PRojects IN Controlled Environments). At the time of writing PRINCE 2 is the current version of PRINCE, though significant revision is due in 2008.[2]

PRINCE provides a comprehensive structure and quality framework which specifies procedures for coordinating people and activities in a project, for how the project is designed, for how it is supervised and what to do if the project develops away from that originally documented. The way in which PRINCE comprehensively specifies roles and processes means that the bureaucratic overhead makes it more suited to medium to large projects than to small ones, though slimmed down versions of the methodology have also been developed.[3]

Many other examples of alternative project methodologies intended for use in particular project contexts can be found through web searches; for example, Rapid Applications Development (RAD) for use in software development projects.

---

[2] http://www.prince2.org.uk/home/home.asp
[3] http://www.prince2passport.com/SPOCE_Mini_Method_V3/PMGuide.html

The project life cycle

The stages of a project's life cycle are indicated in Figure 3.1. In reality the progression through stages may be less clear-cut than is suggested in the figure. For instance, planning and project organisation does not stop when implementation begins and, depending upon how the project develops, there may be a need to revisit aspects of the project's definition during subsequent stages. We will look briefly at each of the main stages in turn.

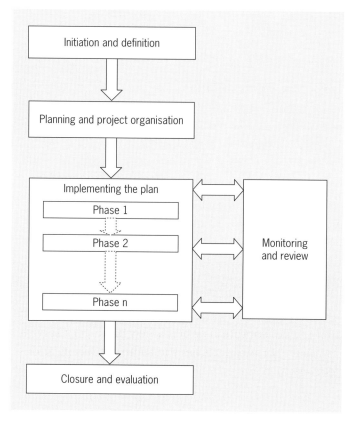

Figure 3.1 *Project life cycle*

Project initiation and definition

Project initiation and definition is critical. A project idea may engender such enthusiasm that during the rush to implement it, the basic definition and proper planning of the project are given scant attention. Many projects fail because they are not properly thought through from the start, so defining what the project entails must be considered in detail at the very beginning of the process.

Whilst we have considered how projects may be initiated as a direct result of an organisation's strategic programme of change, a project may also be initiated for a number of other reasons; for example:

- a request from a potential customer to provide a new service or product
- a customer complaint about poor delivery times
- an internal proposal for a new product or service, or for changes to an existing process
- an agreed view that there must be a better way of doing something.

Large capital projects, for example civil engineering projects, are often preceded by an extensive *feasibility* or *scoping study*. Such a study, if it confirms project viability may set out an initial specification for the project. A feasibility study may also be justified for smaller but complex projects, for which the value of a successful project outcome is not immediately apparent or because there is a need to carry out some initial research into some aspects of the project; for example, into the anticipated market conditions when a new product or service is to be launched, or into whether the technical specifications of a system will be compliant with some particular regulations.

A key outcome from the initiation and definition phase will be a *Terms of Reference* (ToR) document or *project brief*. One of the purposes of this document is to define the scope of the work and the range of activities to be carried out.

The TOR will specify at least the following:

- the project sponsor
- the project customer

- the objectives, scope and budget for the project
- the kind of deliverables expected from it
- the different phases of the project and any milestones or key interim points that the project is looking to achieve.

During the following stage of project planning and organisation further information may be added to the ToR, but any subsequent changes need to be accepted and agreed by all stakeholders so that it provides a clear and indisputable definition of the project.

Many of the activities associated with the following chapters of this book are concerned with preparing components of a ToR document for a project proposal relating to your workplace.

Project planning and organisation

Careful planning is crucial and this must take into account the views and requirements of all the project stakeholders. The focus at this stage is on the clarification, quantification, documentation and organisation of all project details so that a formal project plan can be prepared. Responses are needed to questions that ask:

- What tasks or activities will be carried out to meet the project objectives and how will they be grouped together?
- Who will be responsible for carrying them out?
- What resources will be required?
- In what order will activities be performed, and to what timetable?
- What are the potential risks involved in carrying out the various project activities and how can they best be managed?

A project plan is required to be clear and comprehensive; however, as a project proceeds changes may be needed so that new opportunities can be exploited, but where this is the case, changes must be agreed by all stakeholders, as must any implications for the project's ToR. Care must be taken to ensure that the project does not drift away from mutually agreed outcomes simply because new possibilities were identified (but not agreed), as the project plan or its implementation progresses.

Project implementation

This stage is largely self-explanatory. It is the stage when all the carefully laid out plans are put into effect to create the project reality. However, it is unlikely to be all plain sailing. Because projects include an element of novelty or uniqueness, this will mean that prior experience of some of the project activities will either not exist or be incomplete. However, carrying out an appropriate risk analysis in the planning stage should help to reduce the effect of problems arising.

By this stage, a project team will have been assembled to take forward the project through its implementation and this project team will provide the forum for finding solutions to problems as they arise.

Monitoring and review

If the project is to achieve its objectives against time and budget, it will need to be carefully monitored to check progress against the key dates and milestones that have been identified in the project plan. Few projects run without any hitches so there will be a need to review the plan on a regular basis, deal with any potential and actual problems and make any necessary changes to the plan. Monitoring and review is not a single stage of the project life cycle, but is a more or less continuous activity during each of a project's phases.

Project closure and evaluation

This signals the end of the project, when all the project deliverables can be formally signed off and the team disbanded. It is also the point at which the project itself can be evaluated in terms of the experiences gained, the lessons learned, the successes and failures along the way and the overall outcome of the project and its likely future impact. Lessons learned from a project can add to an organisation's corporate learning and be a valuable resource for future project work.

This would be a good time to work through Activity 3.1

Table 3.1 provides a summary of the various stages in a project's lifecycle.

Table 3.1 *Project life cycle summary*

Stage	Notes
Initiation and definition	Defining what the project will do to meet the required outcome or vision
Planning and project organization	How will the vision be achieved, by whom, by when and at what cost?
Project implementation	Doing it, solving problems, maintaining momentum
Monitoring and review	Checking progress against agreed schedules and costs. Reviewing effectiveness of project activity and resources used
Project closure and evaluation	The project completed, the project vision made reality; the project outcomes accepted, signed off and evaluated. Learning captured for the benefit of future project work

Activity 3.1
Key project activities

Aim of this activity

◆ To review a past workplace project in terms of the phases and key features of the project, how successful it was and what if anything could or should have been approached differently.

Useful resources for this activity

◆ *Change, Strategy and projects at work*

◆ Resources at work

◆ Discussions with colleagues

1. Select a project that you have been involved in or affected by during the past – as recent past as possible.

2. Use the table that follows to indicate what the different stages were and approximately how long each lasted. You may need to refer back to Figure 3.1 to remind you of the main stages of the project lifecycle.

3. Summarise what key activities occurred in each stage.

4. Identify what went well and not so well during the execution of the project. Identify any difficulties or unexpectedly easy achievements that occurred and try to establish why they arose; for example, because key activities were difficult to manage, because unforeseen events created the need to change part of the project specification or because unexpected opportunities arose.

5. Was the project considered successful by yourself and by others? Try to think of the reasons why you or others made this judgement.

6. What aspect of the project could or should have been approached differently and how would this have been likely to affect the success of the outcome?

Project title:			
Stage	Length of time involved	Key activities	Difficulties or easy wins that occurred

Conclusions

What could you take forward to a future workplace project that you were involved in?

Discussion

Thinking about your experiences of a previous project in your workplace may help you to anticipate how future projects will be carried out and what aspects of any future projects you are involved with could present difficulties and challenges. What is important is that you and your organisation learn from past successes, difficulties or downright failures.

4 Project initiation and definition

This is the first phase in any project. During this stage the project idea will be worked up into something which is grounded, feasible and clearly specified. The Terms of Reference (ToR) document provides this focus and will indicate to all the involved parties the size, scope and complexity of the work to be undertaken.

The ToR indicates:

◆ What the project is about. A clear vision of how the project adds value to the organisation, customer or stakeholder group is needed. The scope of the project should be defined clearly because this will determine the resources that are required.

◆ How the project will be delivered. This requires an indication of the broad phases of the project and the milestones or key objectives that will mark progress; also an indication of what will be delivered at key points as evidence of progress (the deliverables) and the resources required to achieve a successful outcome.

◆ Project feasibility. This indicates how the project will be managed to ensure that a successful project outcome is not compromised by the inevitable risks and constraints that will apply. Project feasibility will also be supported (or not) by the initial budget and time estimates.

These all need to be defined and agreement reached with project stakeholders, particularly the customer and the project sponsor.

The following sections focus upon working through the project idea using various techniques and tools to provide inputs to the project ToR.

In this chapter we will also consider the usefulness of undertaking an impact analysis focusing upon the people

If possible you should carry out subsequent activities with reference to a project proposal that relates to your workplace. Activity 4.1 will help you to identify a suitable project idea.

dimensions of the change that the particular project will introduce, though this will not form an explicit input to the project ToR. An impact analysis may be undertaken depending upon the:

◆ change readiness of the organisation(s) involved in the project implementation and the....

◆ likelihood of the project, as a component part of a wider programme of change, being viewed as against the interests of particular individuals or groups of individuals.

By carrying out an impact analysis any potential resistance to change and the problems of obstructive behaviour can be anticipated and appropriate strategies adopted to minimise their effect.

Project stakeholders

Bringing a project to a successful conclusion will depend to a large extent on the goodwill, commitment and cooperation of the different people involved in some way with the project – these are the project stakeholders. A project's stakeholders are all those people and groups who have an interest in and are affected by (though in different ways) the project and its outcomes. They will include customers, suppliers and team members. It is important to identify the project stakeholders so that the reason for their involvement and their likely perceptions and priorities can be taken into account when planning how a project is to be implemented. Table 4.1 identifies stakeholder groups and their roles and responsibilities.

Different project stakeholders will have different levels of involvement and interest in what a project is trying to achieve. Some stakeholders will be active participants while others are more passive observers. Stakeholders will also have different levels of power and influence, so it is important to understand the stakeholder interests and perceptions in order to achieve a successful outcome.

Table 4.1 *Key stakeholders and roles*

Stakeholder	Role
Customer Internal or external person or group who will benefit from the changes brought about by the project	– agrees the objectives of the project and how its success is measured and how and where value is to be added – can dictate how some activities are carried out – provides direction and feedback to the project leader
Project sponsor May initiate the project. Normally a senior staff member who adds to the team's authority	– ensures that the project is of relevance to the organisation – helps to set objectives and constraints – may provide resources for the project – is a major contact point for the customer
Project manager/leader Responsible for achieving the project's objectives and leading and motivating the project team	– motivates and develops the project team – produces a detailed plan of action – keeps project stakeholders informed – monitors progress against plan
Team member May have full or part-time involvement in the project, with a specific set of actions to carry out	– takes responsibility for completing specific activities as set out in the plan – may fulfil a specialised role as an expert, or may be needed only for part of the project
Supplier Provider of materials, products or services needed to carry out the project	– can become very involved with, and supportive of the project – delivers supplies against agreed costs and timescales
Other stakeholder Any of the players in this table, plus anyone else who is interested in, or affected by, the outcome of the project	– can contribute to various stages of the planning process by providing feedback and guidance – may only be involved from time to time, or for a single short period of time

Source: *Adapted from Bruce and Langdon (2000)*

The formation of an effective project team is an important aspect of implementing a project. During the project initiation stage a few people may form a small core team working on the project definition. At a later stage, depending upon the type and scale of the project, the project team is likely to be built up as the project continues through planning stages towards implementation. We shall look at how this is best achieved later. However, as the project team increases in size, the number and diversity of stakeholders is likely to increase.

Gauging support and opposition

A project's stakeholders are likely to include potential supporters and also some people who perceive that a project's outcomes are not aligned to their interests. Potential opponents of the project, who are able to exercise power, or influence the opinions of others, may pose a significant threat to a successful outcome if they are not persuaded of the need for the change or, alternatively, if their influence is not neutralised.

An assessment of the perceptions of project stakeholders should be carried out so that a project leader can anticipate where obstructive behaviour may surface and how best to manage it.

To identify how your stakeholders are likely to view a project, ask yourself which of them:

♦ perceive some benefit to themselves from the success of the project

♦ feel threatened by the project or its likely outcome

♦ are likely to support it openly

♦ are likely to oppose it openly

♦ are likely to support it covertly

♦ are likely to oppose it covertly.

You can also ask:

This would be a good time to work through Activity 4.2

♦ How can particular stakeholders influence the success or failure of the project?

♦ What level of influence can a stakeholder exert?

Driving and opposing forces

There can be many reasons why a good idea fails to make a viable project. For example,

◆ it hasn't been thought through carefully enough: it may require a lot of resources for a limited benefit

◆ someone else has had a similar idea and is already undertaking a similar project

◆ there may be too much demand for internal resources from other competing projects

◆ despite being a good idea, the timing is inappropriate

◆ the commitment of key internal stakeholders is inadequate.

Any project must be able to demonstrate real benefits for the organisation and be consistent with its strategic objectives. For example, there could be a need to increase turnover or productivity, reduce time to market or improve organisational communications. These potential benefits will be forces that help drive the project towards a successful conclusion. However, there may also be opposing forces acting to resist a successful conclusion. Examples here include outdated or inadequate technology, the complexity of key systems, insufficient people with the right skills or lack of solid commitment by management or a key stakeholder group.

A technique called forcefield analysis can be used to help assess the overall picture.

Forcefield analysis

Forcefield analysis is a simple but powerful technique first introduced in the area of social science by Kurt Lewin (1890–1947), a significant pioneer in the area of managing social change. It provides a framework for gauging the effect of factors that influence a situation. Factors are identified and represented as forces that either drive progress towards a goal or as forces that block progress towards its achievement. The technique can be used to gauge how progress towards a successful project outcome is likely to be helped or hindered by the factors that influence the outcome. Carrying out a forcefield analysis can help indicate whether the project has a good overall chance of success, or whether the combined effect of the opposing forces is likely to be too strong. The comparison of the relative strengths of supporting and opposing drivers will also help highlight those areas where some action may be taken to increase the strength of supporting drivers and reduce or negate the effect of opposing drivers.

Figure 4.1 shows in diagrammatic form how driving forces can be represented on one side of the centre line and opposing forces on the other. Drivers are represented in terms of their relative strength with +5 representing a major force supporting the project, with +1 a rather minor supportive force. On the opposing side, –1 would represent a minor opposing force that is not insurmountable, while –5 would represent an opposing force working strongly against the project with a real chance of preventing it reaching a successful outcome. Figure 4.1 is an example based on how driving and opposing forces are likely to impact upon an online trading project.

Figure 4.1 *Forcefield analysis relating to the introduction of online trading*

Discussion of the forcefield analysis – online trading project

In Figure 4.1 the company is subject to strong market pressure to introduce online trading because increasing numbers of customers and suppliers expect this. The threat of new entrants into the marketplace is adding some urgency to the pressure to change. At the same time the company's traditional sales base is declining. All these forces are driving the company towards introducing online trading facilities.

However, on the debit side, the company is a rather traditional one, and extremely wary of change. It has a history of very cautious investment in IT, and has very limited in-house expertise.

In this example, it seems clear that some radical action is called for if the company is to survive. This will involve trying to shift the organisational culture to one which is more open to the opportunities that new technologies can bring whilst also making a substantial capital investment in technology, possibly with the short-term assistance of external IT consultants.

Carrying out a forcefield analysis requires strict objectivity and judgement – neither overly optimistic nor overly pessimistic when gauging either types of force: for example, are all the benefits claimed realistic? Also, looking at the opposing forces, are there any that could be neutralised in order to obtain a better balance in favour of a successful project outcome?

It is important when carrying out such an assessment that all drivers are examined to ensure that they are not repeated articulations of an underlying single factor. It is also possible for a driver to be interpreted as having a driving and an opposing influence at the same time. In this case the net result in the dominant direction should be presented.

This would be a good time to work through Activity 4.3

A proposed project may satisfy the feasibility criteria initially, but it is advisable, as planning progresses, to repeat the analysis to take into account the effect of any new factors or any changes in the significance of existing ones.

During the project initiation stage it is critically important to articulate clearly what the project is aiming to achieve and how this will benefit the organisation, customer or stakeholder group. This is achieved using a project vision statement.

Project vision statement

The vision statement is a clear statement that summarises what benefits the project will bring about, in a way that can be understood by all project stakeholders, particularly those who are charged with making it happen – the project team. Where a project initiative is cascaded directly from a strategic change initiative, the project vision should naturally articulate some aspect(s) of the higher level change vision statement and demonstrate strategic fit by supporting one or more of the strategic objectives.

Figure 4.2 indicates a process that can be used to produce a project vision statement. The project sponsor along with the team will examine what the project is going to achieve and brainstorm what changes may result. Ideas generated should be checked with the project customer (internal or external) to ensure consistent expectations.

Where the customer is external, the customer's own take on the vision may differ because it will be based on their understanding of how the project meets their own organisation's objectives and constraints. There may be occasions when a customer's vision of expected benefits is not realistic, but resolution of differences at this stage will avoid potential disappointment at a later stage in the project's lifecycle.

A good project vision statement, apart from being succinct, should aim to provide a degree of excitement and enthusiasm amongst key stakeholders.

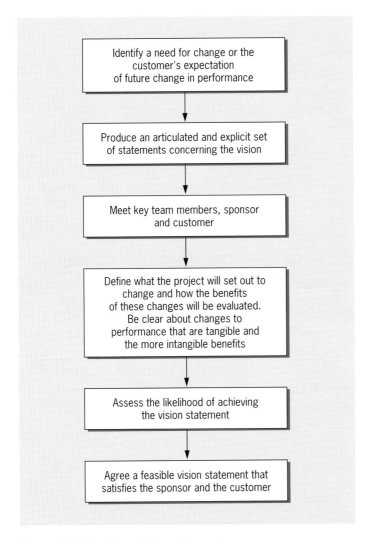

Figure 4.2 *Creating a vision statement*
Source: *Adapted from Bruce and Langdon (2000)*

Case study: Building an extension to your home

Consider how you would prepare a vision statement for building an extension to your home.

A vision statement could express the benefits envisaged from creating a roof garden or indoor swimming pool, or something more modest like a play area for the children

This would be a good time to work through Activity 4.4

or an additional bedroom. The statement would express the outcomes in tangible ways, for example in terms of leisure and utility (additional space and facilities) and possibly less tangibly in terms of pleasure, status, comfort and feelings of well-being. The vision statement provides the picture of what the future will look like in relation to your extended home and its contribution to the enhancement of your family's lifestyle when the project is successfully completed.

Setting objectives

Whereas the vision statement describes the beneficial future state following the successful conclusion of the project, the objectives identify the detailed means of getting there. There may be several key objectives that can help define the route to a successfully completed project. Objectives may coincide with the completion of phases of a project, but this is not a requirement. If they do, they are referred to as 'milestones'.

All stakeholders need to understand, accept and support a project's objectives. Objectives provide a focus on the achievement of results and a way of checking that the project is on target. To be effective, objectives should be SMART; that is they should be:

- ◆ **S**pecific
- ◆ **M**easurable
- ◆ **A**chievable
- ◆ **R**esults-oriented
- ◆ **T**ime-related.

 **SMART**

There are several variations on the SMART acronym, but they are generally consistent in the criteria they specify for the setting of effective objectives.

Supposing an example of an objective is to:

improve the response time for the handling of customer complaints.

As it stands, although it is a specific objective it does not satisfy the other criteria.

In order to test whether, after a particular remedial action, the objective was being achieved, you would need to indicate how the change in performance would be measured. In this case a reduction in the existing average of response times would be a starting point. However, what reduction in response time should be set? A reduction from, for example, 5 working days to 48 hours may suit the purpose, but by what date should that objective be achieved? Specifying tomorrow, would probably be unachievable, compared with the required improvement being achieved over a 2 or 3 week period. The development of the original objective in this way would now satisfy the SMART criteria.

A suitably modified objective could be to:

improve the response time for the handling of customer complaints to a maximum of 48 hours by the 31st December (this year).

Assuming that this was deemed to be achievable, this would now satisfy the SMART criteria.

The project team will need to agree appropriate SMART objectives based on a clear understanding of what needs to be achieved, how progress towards objectives will be measured and what indicators will be used for this purpose.

> **Case study: Building an extension to your home**
>
> Consider how you would now identify objectives for the home extension project. Remember that the purpose of objectives in this context is to map out the route to project completion rather than simply creating a list of features of the completed project.

Objectives for the home extension project could be based on the following events, some of which may be used as project milestones. Each of these could be expressed in terms of quantifiable and dated outcomes so that they become SMART objectives. They are:

♦ architect's plans received indicating how the required floor space and access is to be achieved

♦ bank approves increased mortgage provision

♦ planning and building consent received from local regulatory authorities

♦ contract agreed with builder

♦ external construction completed

♦ internal decoration completed.

Whilst the expressed vision may include several intangible features, this may have implications for setting SMART objectives. For example, for the architect's plans to be completely acceptable they would need to satisfy the expressed vision in terms of both the tangible and the less tangible aspects. Tangible here would be meeting the required increase in floor area. Intangibles might be the feeling of comfort and well-being. Specifying the intangible aspects can be more difficult, especially where different value systems come into play (one person's idea of comfort and well-being may not align with others' perceptions).

Of course functionality in performance is a key part of the vision formation and objective setting processes, but intangibles can be equally important. In many projects, particularly those sponsored by an external customer, failure is often attributed to not having delivered on the difficult-to-specify intangibles.

This would be a good time to work through Activity 4.5

82

Key milestones

Some or all of the identified objectives may be a project 'milestone'. A project milestone is an objective that signifies the completion of a phase of a project and for which there is tangible evidence that this has happened – a project 'deliverable'. From the list of objectives for the home extension project, *planning and building consent received from local regulatory authorities* could mark the successful completion of the planning phase to be followed by a construction phase. The 'deliverable' associated with this milestone would be a formal notification of approval attached to the approved plans. In a work setting some examples of project milestone deliverables are:

◆ a minuted review meeting

◆ an interim report

◆ acceptance sign-off of some newly commissioned equipment.

In summary there is a need to agree a clear project vision statement that everyone can commit to. The route to achieving the project vision should be marked by objectives. Project objectives should be:

◆ aligned with the organisation's strategic objectives

◆ SMART

◆ agreed and accepted by the project team and other stakeholders

In addition,

◆ particular objectives should be agreed as defining project milestones with specified deliverables.

Project scope and framework

In this section we will consider the framework in which a project is defined. The project vision, objectives and milestones must be set within a defining framework. The scope of a project defines the boundaries that apply. First and foremost scope specifies clearly what is to be included in the final project outcome and what is not.

Differing perceptions

I have often been in the situation where I thought I was clear about statements that I had made or that were made by others regarding work that was to be carried out. However, at a later time I found my perception differed to the other party's understanding.

An example is where I've had work done on my car or on my home. In more than one case I recall thinking that some particular aspect of the work was included, yet the contractor claimed that it wasn't. This suggests that the scope of the work (what would be included) was inadequately defined, so the fault could be as much mine as the contractor's.

In project work it is important to ensure that misunderstandings are avoided wherever possible by paying careful attention to the detailed specification of the scope of the work to be carried out.

A failure to define and agreed scope is a common reason why projects run into difficulties. Project scope includes additional considerations beyond the specification of final project deliverables, for example:

◆ a clear understanding of a project's business rationale and its strategic fit

◆ an understanding of the expectations of all the different stakeholders

- detailed agreement about what the project involves and the activities required to complete the project

- the resource implications associated with the work to be carried out (finance, time and materials, human skills and commitment)

- the detailed project outcomes.

At a practical level, some further examples of aspects that may be defined in the scope of the project are:

- the units, departments or branches to be covered by the project, for example marketing and sales only

- the groups of staff to be involved

- location – project activity may be required at one or several locations

- the business processes to be included; for example, sales only

- the products or services involved

- the organisation and authority vested in the project team and the project leadership

- arrangements for project security and confidentiality.

Constraints

From Lake's (1997) definition of a project the specification of time, cost and quality (or performance) are central criteria to the successful outcome of a project. These elements will always have some tension between them. Skimp on cost and the timing may slip or quality suffer; overemphasise quality and costs can escalate.

The time constraints of a project are not always within a project team's control, though the importance of time will vary from project to project. In some cases slippage of several weeks might not matter; in other cases this could be critical and cause a project's customer to seek compensation or activate penalty payment clauses in the project agreement.

Defining the scope and establishing the project framework should enable the required project budget to be estimated. Estimating a project budget is usually achieved in several iterations. During the very early stages the cost implications are usually referred to as 'ball park' estimates. As project definition progresses and the resources and activity implications are specified more clearly, subsequent project cost estimates will be based more on fact than feel, and should therefore attract greater confidence. The eventual approval of a project will depend upon a detailed project budget being agreed with the project sponsor and customer.

Typical questions to ask when developing a project budget

◆ If the project team members are doing a lot of travelling around, will they all need laptop computers? What are the travel costs likely to be?

◆ Will the project team need dedicated workspace?

◆ Will all the necessary skills be in place, or will team members or any others need training to carry out their roles?

◆ Will external consultants need to be employed? (...or to save a consultancy bill can suitable internal sources of expertise be identified?)

◆ Is there any contingency set aside should identified risks become reality?

◆ What existing resources can be made use of to reduce time and costs? For example, another department may have carried out a customer survey which, although not completely up to date, can be used in this project, saving on the commissioning of a fresh one?

Case study: Building an extension to your home constraints

Think about the constraints and deliverables that could affect the home extension project. Cost will clearly be a major constraining factor but there are some others that need consideration:

- Can one company carry out all the work, or will some be contracted out?

- How many people will be employed at any one time?

- Will it require specialist architectural services?

- Time is always important: how long will it take to obtain planning consent? Does some of the work need to be done before winter sets in? What happens if the firm with the best estimate is not available until October?

Deliverables should be specified quantitatively where possible; for example excavation trench measurements, quantities of building materials, quality specifications of materials, detailed installation of services such as water and electricity.

However, there are also likely to be intangible deliverables that are hard to specify. What every project customer would really like to achieve is 100% satisfaction, with no hassle, good humour, lowest cost and the project delivered on time. Tensions usually surface as failure to live up to one or more of these expectations become apparent. Open and frequent communication between parties can help avoid the potential for disputes to arise.

This would be a good time to work through Activities 4.6 and 4.7

In the next section we consider how best we can approach the issue of managing risk in projects.

Project risk analysis

Routine tasks are, by their nature, familiar to us. The outcomes of performing routine tasks are therefore usually highly predictable. Project work by contrast includes elements of risk and uncertainty associated with the uniqueness and unfamiliarity of some of the work or the context in which it is carried out. Murphy's Law expresses a 'tongue-in-cheek' but fallacious certainty of things going wrong, if it is possible for them to go wrong.

Murphy's Law states:

If anything **can** go wrong it **will** go wrong.

Though the law is flawed it usefully emphasises the need to examine risk issues carefully and in advance of work being carried out. We will look at the ways of expressing uncertainty and ways of managing identified risks.

Project watching

Not a year goes past without news reports about the 'failings' of significant projects in the public eye. Failure is a contentious term, because as I have indicated a project can be subject to changes in its specification before it is finally completed. Such changes inevitably incur additional costs or extended duration or changes to the final project outcome. Where such changes have been agreed along the way, then this muddies the waters in terms of defining project success in terms of the original specified outcome and its delivery to budget and time!

The IT for NHS programme in the United Kingdom is a very significant investment that, periodically, is picked up in news reports. This has drawn its fair share of criticism, but is a long duration project or series of projects, so the jury is still out in terms of the successful delivery of all outcomes.

The troubled commissioning of Heathrow's Terminal Five towards the end of March 2008 demonstrated how a high profile and prestigious project can backfire.

The build up to the next Olympic Games too is always a good 'project' to watch, especially in view of the periodic debate about the Games' longer term value to the host nation as the initial cost estimate of hosting the games invariably escalates as the event draws near.

Sources of risk

All the likely risks in a project need to be identified, assessed and managed to maximise the overall likelihood of project success.

For most projects there will be many sources of risk. Assumptions that seem quite reasonable at the start of a project may be proven otherwise if and when conditions in internal or external environments change during the project duration.

Some common areas where risks arise are:

Timing: Project implementation will require the completion of many different activities and their durations are individually estimated. Sometimes it will not be possible to undertake an activity until previous ones have been completed. This often means that delays can cascade throughout an entire project and compound the uncertainties associated with individual activities. Activities involving external suppliers or contractors may be difficult to manage if there is little control by the project team.

Technology: Projects reliant upon newly emerging technologies are likely to be high risk. The newer the technology being used on a project, the greater the uncertainty that it will function as planned. Tried and tested technologies may be preferable for this reason.

People-related: People are often the source of much uncertainty. Human behaviour, for example as a result of misunderstandings or conflicting views, may cause progress to stall. It is essential, therefore, to provide a supportive framework to prepare people for the challenges ahead. Appropriate styles of management and leadership can also help support people who may not feel confident in carrying out unfamiliar roles or tasks. When managers or leaders are observed to be focussing on issues for political purposes this is likely to be perceived as unhelpful and exacerbate any existing tensions.

Finance: Cost over-runs are a major risk. Costs are not solely determined by internal factors; for example, external suppliers may change their prices and the cost of project finance may change if interest rates change.

Customer: One very basic assumption is that what the customer really wants is fully understood and will not change during the project. In reality, there is always the risk of producing a 'successful' project outcome that the customer decides they no longer want.

Identifying and responding to risk

A detailed survey should be carried out to identify all significant sources of risk associated with a project. Risk assessment of each aspect can then be undertaken by querying:

◆ What could possibly go wrong here?

◆ How likely or unlikely is it that things will go wrong?

◆ What impact would it have on the project?

◆ What can be done to avoid or mitigate the risk?

Again, such an exercise is best carried out within a project team environment which includes people who have the relevant knowledge and expertise to underpin the judgements made.

Calculating the probability of success

Uncertainty is expressed by a probability value. Figure 4.3 is concerned with the project to build a house extension. Each phase has a probability value associated with it that expresses the likelihood of that phase being completed successfully. Each probability can take a value between the limits of 1 and 0. A probability value of 1 corresponds to complete certainty of that phase being completed successfully. A probability of 0 corresponds with complete certainty of that phase **not** being completed successfully. In practice probability values will lie somewhere between these two extremes.

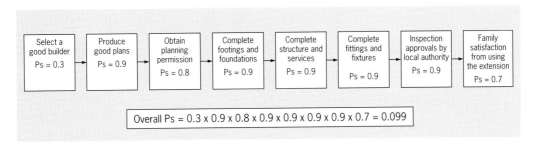

Figure 4.3 *The probability of achieving a successful outcome – home extension project*

In Figure 4.3 each phase is linked in a 'series' fashion. This is appropriate when all the phases must be completed successfully to reach the required end result – a completed project. The calculation of the overall probability of a successful outcome for a project where each phase can be represented in this way is also indicated in Figure 4.3. It simply involves multiplying the probabilities together. Notice that in the sample calculation the overall probability of success has a lower value than the lowest individual value (less than 0.1 overall, compared with the lowest individual value of 0.3). This will always be the case for a set of independent phases (or activities) that can be represented in a series configuration. In fact, if any one of the phases is given a probability close to zero, this would suggest that the project itself is very likely to fail.

Analyses of this sort can be carried out at different levels. Here I have referred to phases in the home extension project, but I could just as easily have referred to all the activities that are required to complete a project or project phase.

In reality analyses of this sort need to be interpreted carefully. My interpretation of the situation represented by Figure 4.3 is not that an extension would be unlikely to be built, but that some significant deviations from the project plan would be needed. The question that could be raised is whether at the end of the process the project outcome would meet the unqualified delight of the project customer, in this case the occupying family.

In addition to risks associated with going ahead with a project, there may well be risks associated with not going ahead with it. This could happen, for example, if a competitive organisation had a similar project idea and was implementing it. Not carrying out a project in this situation could result in a competitive disadvantage, involving for example, the loss of market share.

Contingency planning

One approach to reducing unacceptably high-risk levels is to undertake contingency planning. This involves identifying and preparing alternative ways to complete a particular activity or phase.

In many situations (not necessarily projects) where maintaining a process or service is critical, it is usual to provide a standby arrangement for emergency use. This can be represented by a parallel configuration as shown in Figure 4.4. Here a different approach to calculation is used where the outcome is of a probability value greater than either of the individual values. So by creating an alternative or contingency activity, the likelihood of success is strengthened.

In Figure 4.5 I have added a contingency arrangement to 'produce good plans' by engaging a second architect. This would improve the resulting probability of success of that phase, but this could potentially incur additional delay

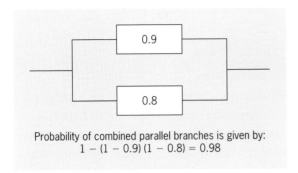

Probability of combined parallel branches is given by:
$$1 - (1 - 0.9)(1 - 0.8) = 0.98$$

Figure 4.4 *Representing contingencies*

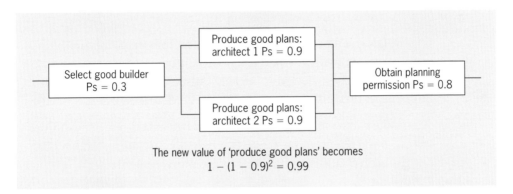

The new value of 'produce good plans' becomes
$$1 - (1 - 0.9)^2 = 0.99$$

Figure 4.5 *Improving the probability of achieving a successful outcome – home extension project*

and increased cost. Arranging contingency for the phases with the greatest levels of uncertainty would contribute the greatest improvement to the likelihood of a successful project outcome. Again, there is a need to interpret the results of such analyses carefully. The analyses are also based on an assumption that activities are independent of each other. This means that the probability of one activity being successful will in no way influence the probability of any other activity being successful.

Strategies for managing risk

The uniqueness of any activities in project work and the pressure to keep to project schedules could lead to levels of risk to people that are not acceptable from either an ethical or health and safety viewpoint. Project teams must ensure that health and safety guidelines and regulations are followed in spirit and substance.

Risk assessments are normally required for any new activity or process whether they are carried out as part of a project or not. Project work generally includes work that involves higher levels of risk than routine operational work. Approval of a project proposal is likely to depend upon evidence that a full risk assessment process has been completed. Not carrying out a proper risk assessment could leave a project team open to potential charges of negligence so it is important that risk assessments are properly recorded.

During a project's life cycle, risk factors may change significantly. A risk register should be maintained and regularly reviewed to identify any changes in the level of specified risk factors or any newly identified ones.

Risk assessment procedures may be carried out in a number of different ways. There will be risks that are specific to the project and also others that are more general.

Specific risks may be associated with each key activity or project phase (depending upon how the project is broken down) and these will need to be identified. Table 4.2 indicates how a list of project-specific risks might be prepared relating to key activities or phases in a project. Even though a

Table 4.2 *Project-specific risk*

Project key activity/ stage	Risk description	Probability of success	Risk category (high, medium, low)	Potential impact of risk (high, medium, low)
Develop software	No in-house experience of using development suite	0.65	High	High
Purchase actuator assembly	Final cost to be confirmed by supplier when system specification is completed. Potential for increased cost	0.8	Medium	Medium
... .				

probability of success may not be quantified, there should be some agreement over whether each risk should be categorised as high, medium or low; here *high* means that the risk is likely to materialise. Where probability values are quantified you might consider that a probability of success between 1 and 0.9 corresponds to a low risk, between 0.7 and 0.9 corresponds to medium risk and any value less than 0.7 as representing a relatively high probability of the risk materialising.

For each risk (high, medium or low) it is also important to consider what would be the impact to the project if indeed that risk event did happen. Again the severity of impact could be classed as high, medium or low, where a high impact suggests a serious threat to a successful project outcome.

In addition to project-specific risks there will also be more general risks, for example, those arising from factors relating to the external context in which the organisation operates. The potential impact of these also needs to be evaluated. Table 4.3 identifies some categories that may be considered, though these are not exclusive.

Table 4.3 *Environmental risks to project success*

General risk categories	Risk category (high, medium, low)	Risk impact (high, medium, low)
Physical – for example, loss of or damage to information, equipment or buildings as a result of accident, fire or natural disaster.		
Technical – for example, systems do not work, or work to specification sufficiently, to deliver the anticipated benefits.		
Labour – for example, key people unable to contribute to the project because of, for example, illness, career change or industrial action.		
Political/social – for example, withdrawal of support for the project as a result of a change in government, a policy change by senior management or public or media protests.		
Liability – for example, threatened or actual legal action.		

The next stage in developing a project risk management strategy is to gather all the risk factors onto the matrix of Table 4.4 to help focus attention on those risks which pose the greatest threat to a successful project outcome and which must therefore be managed effectively. A risk in the top left cell must be managed with great care. A risk in this box means that not only is it likely to happen but also that the consequences would be severe. Other risks having a high to medium impact may also warrant careful management, even if there is a lower risk of them occurring.

Table 4.4 *Aggregation of risks*

		Potential risk impact		
		High	*Medium*	*Low*
Risk probability	High	Possibility of control system technology operating below required specification		
	Medium		Possibility of delivery delays of control system components	
	Low			Promotional material not ready in time

This process that I have described helps to identify those risk factors that should be looked at as a priority (Table 4.5). Having identified which risks warrant serious concern, what are the options for managing them? A variety of risk management strategies may be appropriate.

Table 4.5 *Risk prioritisation*

Priority	Risk description	Management strategy/action to be taken
1	Possibility of preferred control system technology operating below required specification	Contingency – as a fall back measure, investigate possibility of interfacing system to comparable control system from alternative supplier
2	Possibility of delivery delays of control system components	Modify purchasing schedule to order required components earlier
3	... ...	... ...

Risk management strategies

Risk avoidance – for example, you could decide to refuse a contract because the risk is too high for the benefit that could result.

Risk reduction – regular reviews can help to reduce the risk associated with a particular stage of a project. Contingency planning to provide an alternative way forward can help, as also can increasing particular resources available to the project or arranging more flexible working.

Risk protection – taking out insurance against particular eventualities could be sensible for some risks that are not directly manageable.

Risk management – use of written agreements in areas of potential disagreement.

Risk transfer – passing the responsibility for a difficult task within a project to another organisation with more experience in that field – may require the use of external consultants.

This would be a good time to work through Activities 4.8 and 4.9

The following end-of-chapter activities are designed to consolidate your knowledge and learning by applying what you have learnt to your workplace. You can make best use of these activities by using them as the basis for developing a real workplace project proposal that you could take forward. By completing the activities in this and subsequent chapters you should be able to create a ToR document that could be used as the basis of a project proposal in your workplace.

Alternatively, most of the activities can be responded to on the basis of your experiences of projects that are either now well underway or have been completed. If you choose to respond in this manner then you will have the benefit of hindsight, but you should try to resist making easy judgements on this basis and try to perceive what actually happened through the eyes of someone at the time.

This would be a good time to work through Activity 4.10

Activity 4.1
Workplace project idea

Aim of this activity

◆ To identify a workplace project idea.

Useful resources for this activity

◆ Resources at work

◆ Discussions with colleagues.

Use the template below to brainstorm your own project idea. You should try to generate more than one project idea and then chose one that can best meet the criteria in the table that follows.

Template – brainstorm project ideas

Prompts	Responses
What problems and opportunities are you aware of in your work or workplace? Remember that a problem can be an opportunity for innovation.	
What processes or systems in your work area create difficulties or impede the quality of the services or products you or your department provide to others? What processes or systems in your workplace could be beneficially transformed? Try to anticipate what perceptions and priorities other people, such as your customers and line manager, would have here.	
What aspects of your work are of particular interest to you?	
Do you anticipate any obstacles in developing a project plan around any of the ideas that you already have?	

Record your project idea(s) here:

Test criteria for a proposed workplace project

Criteria for project proposal	Notes on how each criterion will be met
The project is of potential benefit to my workplace organisation and supports the organisation's strategic plans.	
The project is at an appropriate level for me to be able to plan and take forward if approved and appears feasible and realistic.	
The proposed work satisfies the criteria for being a project (see Lake's definition, Chapter 3, page 60)	

Activity 4.2
Anticipated stakeholder influence

Aim of this activity

◆ To explore the likely influence of stakeholders in a proposed project (or alternatively, actual influence in a past project)

Useful resources for this activity

◆ *Change, Strategy and projects at work*

◆ Resources at work

◆ Discussions with colleagues.

Complete the table that follows to assess the influence of stakeholders in the project you have chosen to consider. You should refer back to Table 4.1 where the various categories of project stakeholder were identified. Record your responses to the following tasks.

1 For each stakeholder category state what benefits and concerns they are likely to perceive for your project. It may help to ask yourself for each stakeholder category 'What would I stand to gain or lose?' and 'What would be my reaction to the project if I was in their shoes?'

2 Identify each stakeholder as being one of the following:

   ◆ active supporter

   ◆ active opponent

   ◆ covert supporter

   ◆ covert opponent.

3 Assess each stakeholder category's likely level of influence in the project.

Discussion

The interests and perceptions of stakeholders may change as a project progresses, so it is advisable to ensure that you keep informed about their views. Frequent and effective communication is a key factor here.

If you based your response to this activity on a previous project you may have found that the stakeholders exercised more influence (for good or ill) than you had imagined.

Title of project:				
Stakeholder category (Table 4.1, Change, Strategies and Projects at Work)	Stakeholder perceived benefits	Stakeholder perceived concerns	Active/covert supporter or opponent	Level of influence (high, medium, low)

Activity 4.3
Forcefield analysis

Aim of this activity

◆ To evaluate the balance of driving and resisting forces for a proposed project using a forcefield analysis.

Useful resources for this activity

◆ *Change, Strategy and projects at work*

◆ Resources at work

◆ Discussions with colleagues

◆ General news media.

Carrying out a forcefield analysis should provide important evidence to support the business case for a propose project.

Identify the key factors that are most likely to influence (positively or negatively) the successful outcome of your project. You may be able to identify all the relevant factors yourself, but you should also consult with other people in your organisation, including some of the potential stakeholders where possible; they may be able to suggest important key factors that should be included.

Depending upon the nature of your project proposal, newspaper reports (especially business features or business focused newspapers), library or web searches, statistical information from governmental sources and so on may provide you with further insights into the factors that should be included. You should continue your efforts until you feel confident that you have created a realistic list of key factors.

1 List the key factors that you have determined from your investigations in the left-hand column of the following table.

Identification and evaluation of driving and resisting forces

Key factors for the proposed project:	Driving force (+) or resisting force (−)	Strength of force (1–5)

2 For each factor that you have identified, establish whether it is an effective driving force (one that is likely to work towards your project being successful) or a resisting force (one that is likely to work against your project being successful). Indicate this by including a + or a − in the middle column.

3 Now evaluate the strength of the forces that are working for or against your project using values between 1 and 5. Use 1 for a weak force (driving or resisting) and 5 for a strong force (driving or resisting). Use the right-hand column to enter the value for each of the driving forces.

4 Complete your forcefield analysis for your project proposal by drawing bars across appropriate cells of the following template taking care to label each bar to show which force it represents.

Forcefield analysis template

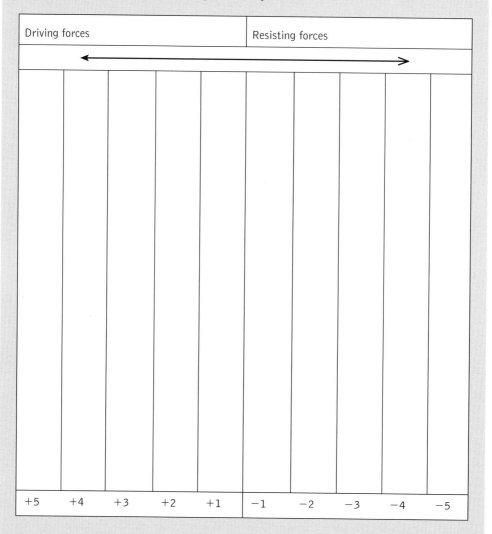

Driving forces					Resisting forces				
+5	+4	+3	+2	+1	−1	−2	−3	−4	−5

5 Write a short summary indicating how you interpret the results of your analysis. Do the results of your analysis suggest any additional actions that could reinforce the chance of the project succeeding?

◆ Summary and interpretation:

◆ Action needed: (if any)

Discussion

It is possible that your forcefield analysis could expose some strong resisting factors of which you were previously unaware.

Activity 4.4
Vision statement template

Aim of this activity

◆ To create a vision statement relating to your project proposal.

Useful resources for this activity

◆ *Change, Strategy and Projects at Work*

◆ Resources at work

◆ Discussions with colleagues.

Follow the process indicated in figure 4.2 of *Change, Strategy and Projects at Work* to create a vision statement for your workplace project. Make use of the notes that follow in relation to each box in the figure. Where possible you should consult with your workplace colleagues, customers and other stakeholders including your project sponsor if you have taken the step of introducing your proposal to your workplace.

Step 1. You should already have identified a change that you wish to introduce.

Step 2. Write a few lines indicating what you are setting out to achieve. Some short examples are:

◆ to significantly improve patient waiting time at a GP surgery

◆ to increase the provision of skills training in a government office

◆ to manufacture the world's fastest network switch.

Notice that these statements do not inform how the vision will be achieved. This is the job of the project objectives.

Step 3. Where possible you should meet with and discuss your ideas with your project sponsor and other potential stakeholders and make a note of their concerns and priorities.

Step 4. You may need to develop further your ideas relating to the benefits that your project could bring to your organisation. The issue of how such benefits can be evaluated is important too. This is because business improvements might arise for other non-connected reasons, so you need to state how any improvements could be evaluated (preferably measured) and correctly attributed to your project. You will need to present and justify your ideas later to stakeholders and colleagues, so it is well worth thinking deep and hard about these aspects.

Step 5. Your forcefield analysis that you carried out in Activity 4.3 should provide the information needed here.

Step 6. After carrying out this process and taking account of any areas of concern expressed by stakeholders or colleagues you should be able to develop a suitable vision statement for your project that satisfies both the project sponsor and the customer.

Express your final and agreed vision statement in the template that follows. It should be brief and written in a style that can be readily understood and **visualised** by all workplace colleagues and stakeholders.

Title of project:	
Statement:	
Agreed with:	Stakeholder role:
Dated:	

Activity 4.5
Developing SMART project objectives

Aim of this activity

◆ To create SMART objectives for your proposed project (or alternatively to review objectives from a past project to determine whether they were SMART).

Useful resources for this activity

◆ *Change, Strategy and projects at work*

◆ Resources at work

◆ Discussions with colleagues

You should feel sufficiently confident to develop a set of objectives for your proposed project and then discuss them with your project sponsor and other colleagues. You may need to refine your objectives based on any feedback you receive.

The number of objectives that you identify could depend on the scale of your proposed project though you should be able to identify a minimum of four or five SMART objectives for any project.

Complete the table that follows using it to restate your vision statement (where you want to be) and to list and check your SMART objectives (how to get there). If you are following this activity on the basis of a past project rather than a project proposal, you will need to find out what the project objectives were and then identify whether they were SMART or not. If they were not SMART were there any implications for the success of the project?

Date:						
Title of project:						
Vision statement:						
Objectives	Description	S	M	A	R	T
1		☐	☐	☐	☐	☐
2		☐	☐	☐	☐	☐
3		☐	☐	☐	☐	☐
4		☐	☐	☐	☐	☐
5		☐	☐	☐	☐	☐
6		☐	☐	☐	☐	☐

Activity 4.6
Project constraints

Aim of this activity

◆ To identify and define constraints that apply to your proposed project.

Useful resources for this activity

◆ *Change, Strategy and Projects at Work*

◆ Resources at work

◆ Discussions with colleagues.

Complete the table below adding any additional factors that you think would be significant in defining a working framework for your project.

Prompt	Your response
What units departments or branches will be involved in the project, for example, would only marketing and sales be involved?	
Which groups of staff will be involved, for example, would call handlers and dispatch staff be included?	
In which location will the project activity take place, for example, would activity be restricted to just one region?	
What business processes will be involved, for example, sales only?	
What products will be affected, for example, would the project be limited to insurance and pensions services, or would it include mortgages?	
What limitations would there be on your freedom to make decisions, for example, on the use of resources and people?	
What freedom would you have to contact outside groups and access information, for example, would commercial confidentiality be crucial?	
Now add any considerations that you think should be included for your particular project.	

Activity 4.7
First project cost estimate

Aim of this activity

◆ To produce an initial estimate of costs for your proposed project.

Useful resources for this activity:

◆ *Change, Strategy and projects at work*

◆ Resources at work

◆ Discussions with colleagues.

You should ask your colleagues and, where possible, people within your finance department about estimating the cost of carrying out your project. You should emphasise that this is a first cost estimate (rather than the more detailed estimate needed before a project can be authorised). The costs needing to be included in a first estimate could include:

◆ equipment costs

◆ cost of any materials or consumables used

◆ labour costs – project staff as well as any others who will be involved in carrying out activities on the project

◆ costs of bought-in services (design, consultancy, installation services and so on)

◆ travel and subsistence costs.

Think about what the main areas of project cost are likely to be for your proposed project. List them against cost categories, using a customised version of the table below as necessary. Find out the level of cost involved for each item that you list. You are not expected to produce accurate costs at this stage because your project ideas will still be developing, but you should be able to anticipate for instance, where a cost is likely to be closer to £1000 or £500.

Cost category	Identified items under each category	Estimated cost
Equipment		
Materials and consumables		
Labour		
Bought-in services		
Travel and subsistence		
Total estimate		

Activity 4.8
Project risk analysis

Aim of this activity

◆ To identify and evaluate risks relating to your proposed project.

Useful resources for this activity

◆ *Change, Strategy and projects at work*

◆ Resources at work

◆ Discussions with colleagues

◆ General news media.

1 List the key activities or the main stages of your proposed project in the following table and then carry out the following. For each key activity (or stage) ask yourself what could go wrong, what the risks are in each case and express the probability of successfully completing that activity as a value between 0 (no prospect of successfully completing) and 1 (certainty of successfully completing).

2 Next categorise each key activity as being of high, medium or low risk by using the following arbitrary ranges:

◆ probability of success less than 0.7 equates to high risk

◆ probability of success between 0.7 and 0.9 equates to medium risk

♦ probability of success of more than 0.9 equates to
  low risk.

Whilst this approach is necessarily simplistic, it should enable you
to categorise the main project-specific risk factors.

3 Complete the first three columns (but not the right-hand
  column yet). Remember that this is an initial risk assessment
  which you will be able to revisit and refine as you develop your
  project plan.

Project-specific risk

Project key activity/ stage	Risk description	Probability of success	Risk category (high, medium, low)	Impact of risk (high, medium, low)

You have focussed so far upon the probability of success in completing specific stages of your project. However, there will also be wider issues (the big picture) that can affect the likelihood of success of your project and these also need investigating and evaluating.

4 The following table identifies some broad areas of potential risk that also need to be examined. Identify which categories of risk could apply significantly to your proposed project by completing the table with the exception of the right-hand column.

Broad areas of risk

Broad risk categories	Extent of risk to your project (high, medium, low)	Impact of risk (high, medium, low)
Physical – for example, loss of or damage to information, equipment or buildings as a result of accident, fire or natural disaster.		
Technical – for example, systems do not work or work to specification sufficiently to deliver the anticipated benefits.		
Labour – for example, key people unable to contribute to the project because of, for example, illness, career change or industrial action.		
Political/social – for example, withdrawal of support for the project as a result of a change in government, a policy change by senior management or public or media protests.		
Liability – for example, threatened or actual legal action.		

Planning how to manage or at least mitigate the risks that you have identified will depend not only upon the probability of that risk materialising, but also on its impact on the project if it does materialise; for example a high-impact risk would suggest a very significant effect on the project outcome whereas a low-impact risk would suggest a marginal effect on the project outcome.

5   For each of the project specific risks and the broad risk categories that you have identified evaluate what impact level would apply should the associated risk materialise. Fill in the right-hand columns of each table accordingly.

In the next activity you will consider how best to manage the risks that you identified.

Activity 4.9
Risk management strategy

Aim of this activity

◆   To develop a risk management strategy for your proposed project.

Useful resources for this activity

◆   *Change, strategy and projects at work*

◆   Resources at work

◆   Discussions with colleagues.

(a) Aggregation of risks:

Use the following matrix to aggregate the risks you identified in Activity 4.8 and that would threaten the success of your proposed project. Categorise each risk according to its area of low/medium/ high risk and low/medium/high impact.

Matrix – aggregation of risks

		Risk impact		
		High	Medium	Low
Risk probability	High			
	Medium			
	Low			

(b) Strategies for dealing with risk:

Refer to the box headed *Risk management strategies* in *Change, strategy and projects at work,* then complete the table that follows to indicate for your proposed project, which areas of risk you think should be prioritised (include high to medium probability and high to medium impact) and what risk management strategy could be adopted in each instance.

Risk prioritisation

Priority	Risk description	Management strategy/action to be taken
1		
2		
3		
4		
5		
6		

Discussion

A risk register should be maintained and regularly reviewed throughout a project's life cycle. Changes in the level of threat or any new risk issues may prompt a change in the way project risk is managed.

Activity 4.10
Terms of reference

Aim of this activity

◆ To assemble an initial project Terms of Reference document for your proposed work-based project.

Useful resources for this activity

◆ *Change, Strategy and projects at work*

◆ Resources at work

◆ Discussions with colleagues

◆ Previous activities for this chapter.

A project Terms of Reference document brings together important information prepared during the project initiation phase. Complete the table below using your responses to previous activities in this chapter. You are advised to use your computer to construct a similar table so that you can expand each entry as needed.

Title of project:	
Project sponsor	
Customer	
Vision statement	
Objectives	
Limitations, exclusions, constraints	
Overall budget	
Resources required	

Deliverables	
Project phases and milestones	
Project risks	
Project staffing: roles and responsibilities	

Discussion

The completion of a project Terms of Reference document (even a version 1) for a project proposal is a significant achievement.

5   Project planning

Following on from the definition of what a project is about as defined by its scope and the constraints that apply, this chapter looks at the detailed planning of its implementation. Whilst careful planning is a prerequisite of a successful project outcome, this is not to say that plans will not need changing as a project is implemented. The planning process itself should expose the project to critical challenge resulting in the surfacing of potential problems that could otherwise arise during the implementation phase. This in turn enables early consideration of alternative courses of action.

Planning begins by breaking down the complete package of work necessary to complete all of a project's objectives into a comprehensive list of activities or tasks. (Note that the terms *activities* and *tasks* are used interchangeably in project management.) Activities are identified at a level of detail that is appropriate for the scale of the project. Next, activity durations and the order in which they are to be carried out to meet the project objectives can be determined to establish the project schedule. Following this, responsibilities for carrying out, or alternatively, overseeing, the activities can be assigned to various people and all other necessary resources allocated.

A strong project team, with a blend of people, skills and experience, is an essential platform for project success. During the initiation of a project, the project team may have consisted of only a few members – perhaps two or three. However, as full planning then implementation gets underway an extended project team will be needed; one which includes individuals with the required mix of expertise, skills and experiences. In addition, an effective team will require a mix of 'team roles'. We shall explore this aspect next before going on to consider some of the tools and techniques used to plan a project.

Building a project team

Although team consensus is generally a good idea, a team where all the thinking and proposed action is stimulated from a restricted number of roles is often deficient and unbalanced and therefore potentially unsound. Effective teams are those in which members contribute a wide range of perspectives and demonstrate different preferences for action. You will always need, for example, someone who is prepared to challenge woolly thinking, someone who will monitor quality, someone who makes sure that team efforts are co-ordinated.

However, it is frequently not possible to pull a team together that is completely balanced and gaps in team roles may occur, as may also repeats of a particular role type. For example, you may have too many technical specialists, who try to narrow the team's focus to their own technical preoccupations, or several members who generate lots of ideas but never implement anything. Most people have attributes and preferences that align with one or more team roles. Some people may be able to compensate for specific roles if these are missing from the team composition, though of course, it helps if they already possess some of the characteristics of the missing role type; there is no point in trying to substitute for a missing 'creative ideas person' with someone whose main team role focus is on ensuring that processes are undertaken correctly and recorded meticulously.

Establishing the roles present and missing in a proposed project team is important and it can also be a good team-building exercise in itself. If each team member is able to recognise the value of their own and others' contributions there is a better chance that the team will be able to work together productively from the start.

Team roles

Meredith Belbin[1] defined a team role as 'a tendency to behave, contribute and interrelate with other team members

---

[1] www.belbin.com

in a particular way'. Within a team, each member will display characteristics associated with one or more of the defined team role types, whether they are aware of this or not.

Belbin and associated researchers undertook a study of managers from all over the world over a period of several years. They were primarily interested in the development of effective management teams. The subjects undertook psychometric tests and were studied for their behaviour within teams of varying composition. Over time, different characteristics and behaviours of team members were observed and distinct role categories were identified. Nine clear team roles emerged which were grouped and named as follows:

- action-oriented roles: shaper, implementer and completer finisher
- people-oriented roles: co-ordinator, teamworker and resource investigator
- cerebral roles: plant, monitor evaluator and specialist.

Each of these team roles was seen to offer a unique contribution to a management team. Along with each role's key strengths, Belbin also identified what he called the 'allowable weaknesses' of each role, which a team needed to be aware of so that it could be managed, or at least, accommodated. Table 5.1 describes Belbin's roles in a little more detail.

Table 5.1 *Belbin's team role types*

Team role type	Contributions	Allowable weaknesses
Plant	Creative, imaginative, unorthodox Solves difficult problems	Ignores incidentals Too preoccupied to communicate effectively
Co-ordinator	Mature, confident A good chairperson Clarifies goals, promotes decision-making, delegates well	Can be seen as manipulative Offloads personal work

Source: *www.belbin.com*

Table 5.1 (*Continued*)

Team role type	Contributions	Allowable weaknesses
Monitor evaluator	Sober, strategic and discerning Sees all options, judges accurately	Lacks drive and ability to inspire others
Implementer	Disciplined, reliable, conservative, efficient Turns ideas into practical actions	Somewhat inflexible Slow to respond to new possibilities
Completer finisher	Painstaking, conscientious, anxious Searches out errors and omissions Delivers on time	Inclined to worry unduly Reluctant to delegate
Resource investigator	Extrovert, enthusiastic, communicative Explores opportunities Develops contacts	Over-optimistic Loses interest once initial enthusiasm has passed
Shaper	Challenging, dynamic, thrives on pressure Has the drive and courage to overcome obstacles	Prone to provocation Ignores people's feelings
Teamworker	Co-operative, mild, perceptive and diplomatic Listens, builds, averts friction	Indecisive in crunch situations
Specialist	Single-minded, self-starting, dedicated Provides knowledge and skills in rare supply	Contributes only on a narrow front Dwells on technicalities

Whilst Belbin's system is used by many Human Resource departments, the approach is not without criticism, these being mainly focused on the business school environment in which many of the observations and experiments were conducted.[2] There are alternative systems aimed at identifying similar team role types; one is included in the activities for this chapter, should you wish to investigate your own team-role type profile.

---

[2] http://encyclopedia.thefreedictionary.com/Meredith+Belbin

Development of team processes

Team development is an important aspect of project working. However, a team newly brought together, where a majority of team members have not previously worked together, needs some time to develop to its optimum effectiveness.

Tuckman and Jenson (1977) suggested that people working together as a group will go through various stages in group development. These are:

Forming: This stage involves introductions and explorative communications – listening to each other and probing others' opinions in some way. In this stage group members are finding out about other group members as well as about the task.

Storming: Here group members may discuss methods of achieving the task that the group is to address and how the group will conduct itself. Differences in approach are likely to surface and group members are likely to consider alternative approaches. This stage is likely to be characterised by the expression and management of differences.

Norming: At this stage the group can now establish agreement about the task, the way in which it will be achieved and about how the group will conduct itself. The group establishes its procedures, norms and values upon which action will be based.

Performing: The group is now ready for focussing on the task to be carried out.

The idea of a group's stages of development is generally useful and provides an acknowledgement of the validity of the expression of differences in approach. A degree of conflict, of questioning and querying the way forward is a natural characteristic of group development.

Additional factors may affect group performance. For instance a group size which is large includes a wider mix of skills, but less opportunity for individuals to participate. Group sizes beyond about ten may therefore be less effective. Optimum group sizes for many smaller projects may be around six people.

The nature of the task in hand is another factor. Groups undertaking tasks with clear and unambiguous objectives can respond more quickly compared with situations where tasks are more open ended. Groups must also be afforded, the resources and support required to undertake their work and given full recognition for their work and achievements. Group composition is important because where several or all members have the same perceptions, outlooks and priorities there may be less conflict and an easier decision-making process, but also less scope for the healthy challenge that can foster innovation.

Teams are groups of people who work interdependently on a common task and with common goals towards a collective outcome. An effective team is characterised by a balance of team roles, by the synergy and commitment of its members and the ability to create innovative solutions to problems that an individual working alone would be unlikely to achieve. Team effectiveness is dependent upon how teams are constructed and managed, particularly in terms of encouraging a high quality of interaction within them. Synergy is generated where team members are clear about their goals and they listen actively to the contributions of others. Due attention is given to social processes and there is a willingness to engage in constructive disagreement. The prerequisites for gaining the commitment of team members are to ensure that team members feel fully included and that their contributions are valued. In a project context this requires frequent, effective and supportive communication between project teams, their leaders and other project stakeholders, particularly those engaged with managing change at the strategic level.

This would be a good time to work through Activities 5.1 and 5.2

Work breakdown structure

A work breakdown structure (WBS) is a hierarchical listing of all the activities needed to complete a project. Figure 5.1 provides an example of a WBS relating to a project *Improvement of Delivery Times*. For the part of the project shown, four phases with associated objectives have been identified. These are shown at the first breakdown level of the hierarchy (below the project title) as:

◆ project startup

◆ gather information

◆ analyse data and develop options

◆ final report.

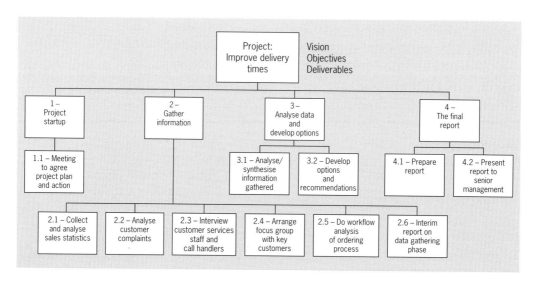

Figure 5.1 *Part of a Work Breakdown Structure (WBS)*

The completion of each of these phases requires a set of one or more activities to be completed. These are shown at the second level of breakdown; for example, under *'Gather information'* the activity *'Analyse customer complaints'* is referenced as 2.2.

Further activity detail can be added by extending the structure where needed. For example, Activity 3.1 *Analyse/ synthesise information gathered* could be divided into: Activity 3.1.1 *Customer views* and Activity 3.1.2 *Staff views*, and subdivided further if, for example, customer views by market segment were required, or if it was felt necessary to analyse the information gathered from different groups of staff as separate tasks. A large complex project may require a WBS having many layers to sufficiently specify all activities to the required level of detail.

One individual may not be able to identify all project activities to a sufficient level of detail so developing the WBS should be carried out by a project team using either a top down or bottom up approach. In the top down approach, the team looks at each of the project objectives that constitute a phase of the project and identifies the main activities to be carried out. Each of these main activities is critically examined to determine whether it warrants a more detailed breakdown. Any further activities that are identified at a lower level can themselves be scrutinised until a satisfactory level of activity definition is achieved. In the bottom up approach, the team may attempt, through brainstorming, for example, to identify all the detailed activities needing to be carried out and then attempt to group them into higher level activities and ultimately phases of the project.

In exploring and defining the project WBS it is useful to highlight the project milestones that will be associated with particular objectives and deliverables, usually marking the end of specific project phases. The project deliverables associated with milestones provide the visible and indisputable evidence that a milestone has been achieved. In Figure 5.1 task 2.6 signifies the end of the data-gathering phase. The deliverable is the interim report.

Useful checks to ensure that the WBS is fit for purpose include:

◆ Do the activities listed in the WBS reflect the priorities set for achieving each objective and, if they are all completed, will the project's objectives be met?

◆ Are all the activities defined in sufficient (or too much) detail?

◆ Are any redundant activities listed or are they all needed?

When a WBS has been completed to an appropriate level of detail it can be used to create Statements of Work that define the work to be carried out for each activity, before responsibility for carrying out the work is allocated to appropriate people or departments. The hierarchical numbering shown as in Figure 5.1 is useful for referencing each activity unambiguously.

In summary, a WBS is used to:

◆ break down complex tasks into smaller manageable components

◆ ensure that every aspect of project activity has been included and covered adequately and that there are no gaps

◆ enable a detailed schedule of activities for each phase and for the whole project to be established

This would be a good time to work through Activity 5.3

◆ identify and plan the resources needed and provide a realistic basis for estimating project costs

◆ allocate responsibilities for tasks to specific individuals or groups.

Resource planning

Each of the activities identified in the WBS must be resourced adequately. Figure 5.2 provides a useful aid for thinking about the key resources needed in a project (Bruce and Langdon, 2000). Resource planning identifies the type, amount and cost of the resources needed for each activity. Providing that the WBS is comprehensive then aggregating the resources for all project activities will provide a summary of the project resources required to carry these out. However, additional resources above and beyond those needed for carrying out project activities will be required, but we will return to these additional requirements shortly.

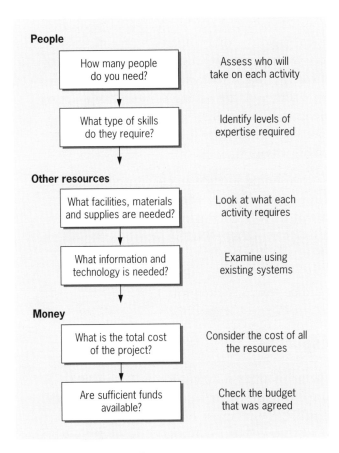

Figure 5.2 *Considering key resources*

People

People are clearly a major resource (and cost) to any project but the apportionment of human resources to a project is unlikely to be straight forward. Estimates of time commitment must be realistic. Where a project activity or series of activities is not expected to require 100% of an individual's time, resource planning will need to distinguish between the elapsed time associated with activities and the actual time commitment required, assuming that when not usefully engaged in the current project's activities, people are gainfully engaged elsewhere.

The way in which the cost of people are included in a project budget will depend upon the sector. For example, there will be wide variations between how projects are costed within an educational organisation compared with a manufacturing organisation. In the manufacturing sector standard costs may be routinely charged to particular activities or sequences of activities, a standard rate having been set based upon past experiences of undertaking similar work within the organisation. This is less likely to be appropriate to an educational organisation.

A project's costs should include an element to reflect the costs associated with the project team, whether or not the team members are undertaking any of the identified activities identified in the WBS. The principle that normally applies here is that people who are working in a project environment are not working full time in their normal roles and so should be costed to the project.

Other resources

These can come in many different forms. For example, a substantial travel budget may be needed, the hire of facilities for a focus group, the purchase of a dedicated piece of equipment for the project, the hiring of external consultants or the translation of a final report for dissemination to an overseas branch. An organisation's internal knowledge resources may be used, for example, to provide training to cover any identified gaps in the skills or knowledge requirements. Internal resources may be more economical and match requirements more closely than using external training sources.

Where outside contractors or consultants are to be used for any part of a project several quotations from a range of providers may need to be sourced. A formal tendering procedure may be required accompanied by a clear ToR document.

Money

Each organisation is likely to have its own preference for costing project work. For example, an absolute costing approach requires all costs to be allocated to a project even if they related to the use of existing equipment not currently being used by others. A marginal costing approach focuses on the additional costs of carrying out project work. Use of some existing equipment would then only be charged to a project if its use was required for another purpose at the same time.

Another area of different interpretation could be whether the inclusion of a training cost should be included in a project budget. This may depend upon whether the particular skills to be acquired are needed specifically for the project or were widely applicable to a range of work contexts.

The charging of overhead costs to a project may also be required. For instance, project administration and the wider provision of facilities will contribute to the true costs of undertaking project work, just as they would be in normal day-to-day work. Finally a contingency provision may be added. This should be made explicit rather than being used to inflate individual resource requirements.

This would be a good time to work through Activity 5.4

In principle, a project budget estimate can be developed by first aggregating all the costs associated with the total project activity and then adding costs that are not specifically associated with activities in the WBS.

How a budget is prepared and presented may be prescribed by the organisation. Costs may need to be presented in a categorised form to comply with organisational requirements. An example of a layout to bring together a project budget estimate is indicated in Figure 5.3. In this example, the WBS activity detail is not apparent, though some typical cost categories are.

However the budget required is estimated, a budget target may already have been set and if so, any budget estimate that exceeds this may cause the project's viability to be questioned, should additional funding not be available. Questions may need to be asked in terms of:

◆ Is there a cheaper way of carrying out any of the activities?

This would be a good time to work through Activity 5.5

◆ How essential is each activity?

◆ Is the right person doing it?

◆ Have all the additional resources needed been identified?

Cost category	Notes	Project requirements	Estimated cost
Hardware	Existing (in-house), bought or leased? If existing internally what charge would be likely? Maintenance agreement needed?		
Software	Number of licences required.		
Other equipment	Existing, bought or leased? If existing internally what charge would be likely? Maintenance agreement needed?		
Project staff	Recruitment costs if new Staff costs – make sensible estimates of the rates that could be charged by your organisation (include on-costs and overheads). Staff may need to be seconded from other departments. Overtime working?		
External staff (e.g., consultants)	Daily rate or fixed fee?		
Travel costs (where appropriate)	Internal and external staff		
Staff development	Training required at each project stage. On site, on-line, or away from workplace?		
Office overheads	Chargeable items such as heating, telephones, security, room hire, postage and so on.		
Hospitality	Costs associated with catering for meetings or training events		
Materials and consumables	Stationery, printer cartridges and so on		
External services or facilities	For example, design studio or advertising agency		
Contingency	What is a reasonable contingency bearing in mind the uncertainties in the proposed project?		
Total estimated costs			

Figure 5.3 *Example framework for a project budget estimate*
Source: *Adapted from JISC infoNet Project Management www.jiscinfonet.ac.uk*

The commitment matrix

The work carried out in the detailed planning so far
described can be brought together in a commitment matrix
which links each activity with a person who is responsible
for ensuring that activity is carried out, the person who
is involved in performing that activity (if different), any
particular needs such as training required, the facilities,
equipment or materials resources required and the estimated
cost of successfully completing the activity. An example of
the sort of entries needed is shown in Table 5.2.

> This would be
> a good time to
> work through
> Activity 5.6

Table 5.2 *Commitment matrix*

Activity	People			Resources				Cost
	Who is responsible?	Who is involved?	Training needs	Facilities	Equipment	Materials		
2.1	RMJ (1 day)	N M (2 days)	Costing techniques (RMJ 1 day)	Syndicate room (2 days)	Data projector (2 days)	Case study material	£1150	
2.2	... ...							

Project network techniques

In previous sections we have looked at what needs to be
done to achieve the objectives of a project. Next we consider
the interdependencies of activities, the order in which they
need to be carried out and the consequences for the time to
project completion.

Activities and dependencies

Network diagrams are used in project working to express the
interrelationships (or dependencies) between activities and to
identify the minimum project duration. Some activities may
need to be carried out in a specific order, with a particular

activity only being allowed to start when others have been completed. For example, in redecorating a room, any wall surface preparation would need to be completed before a fresh coat of paint was applied. On the other hand, some activities, (sanding down a door or a window frame) may be carried out independently of others, allowing these activities to be carried out simultaneously. Dependent activities in the context of this section, are those which rely upon a previous activity (or activities) being completed (or at least started).

The following questions should be asked to investigate the degree of dependency of an activity on others:

* What must be done before this activity can start?
* What can be done once this activity finishes?

A third question can be asked to identify those activities that have a degree of independence from each other:

* What other activities can be done at the same time as this activity?

Identifying activities that can be carried out simultaneously can help to shorten the time taken for a project to be completed.

Some activities may be neither fully dependent on others nor fully independent but this will become clearer when we have looked at some examples.

Asking the preceding questions for each activity should establish the type of dependencies that exist between activities. This can then be expressed in an activity network diagram. An activity network diagram (or just network diagram) in the context of project working is a graphical representation of the sequence of the activities required to complete each phase or the entire project. Each activity is identified using, for example, its WBS reference. The order in which activities are to be completed is, by convention, identified by reading from left to right.

There are two widely used conventions for creating network diagrams. One is referred to as Activity on Arrow (AoA) and the other as Activity on Node (AoN).

It is useful to develop a familiarity with using both representations because:

◆ each form of network diagram has benefits and drawbacks

◆ if you use project planning software in the future you will need to be able to work with the convention adopted by the software application

◆ you may change workplaces and you may need to present network diagrams to project teams that are familiar with one style of presentation only.

AoA network diagrams

In an AoA network diagram each arrow represents an activity. In Figure 5.4 no attempt is made to draw the arrows to scale so a small simple activity could be shown the same size as a longer, more complex activity. In this convention each end of an arrow has a node, usually shown as an open circle with a reference number within it. The node at the arrow head end is the finishing node for that activity and the node at the other end is the starting node. Activities are sometimes referenced using the start and end node references. For example, in Figure 5.4 Activity A could be denoted Activity 1.2. However, it is preferable, where possible, to use the WBS reference along with a descriptive name to ensure easy identification without needing to cross reference.

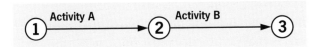

Figure 5.4 *AoA representation of project activities*

Some points to note:

◆ The flow of activities follows the convention of left to right.

- ◆ The node number at the head of the arrow is always higher that the node number at the tail of the arrow.

- ◆ The activities that join at nodes are dependent activities. For example, in Figure 5.4 Activity B cannot start until Activity A has been completed.

- ◆ Nodes need not be numbered in strict sequence; gaps in the numbering can be left so that additional nodes can be added later without having to amend the whole network diagram.

Figure 5.5 shows how an AoA network diagram could be used to represent a tea break. The activities *cut cake* and *make tea* can proceed independently and in parallel. However, the activity *wash up* is shown as dependent upon finishing both *drink tea* and *eat cake*.

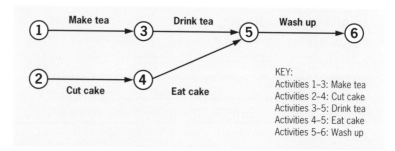

Figure 5.5 *AoA representation of tea break*

Dummies

In the example in Figure 5.5 *drink tea* and *eat cake* have different tail nodes but the same head node. A rule applicable to AoA diagrams is that an activity must not have common tail and head nodes. For example if, no preparation of tea or cake was needed, they were simply ready to consume, then it could be tempting to represent *drink tea* and *eat cake* as in Figure 5.6. However this would breach the rule. Adding a dummy activity as shown in Figure 5.7 (activity reference 2–3) circumvents the problem. A dummy activity is one which is added to complete the logic in an AoA network. A dummy activity has zero time duration.

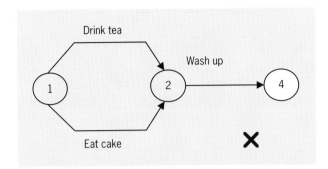

Figure 5.6 *Incorrect representation of modified tea break*

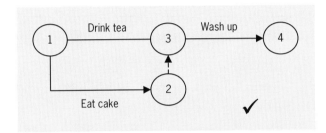

Figure 5.7 *Use of dummy activity (2–3) to satisfy AoA rules*

The time needed to complete an activity is shown under the arrow in consistent time units; for example, days or weeks.

Figure 5.8 shows an AoA network representing activities from the project *Improve Delivery Times* of Figure 5.1.

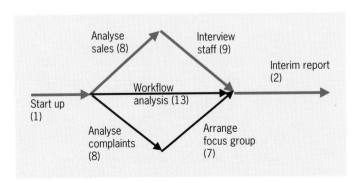

Figure 5.8 *AoA network diagram for project to improve delivery times*

The project duration is the shortest time in which the entire project can be completed. This is defined by the critical path which is shown in blue in Figure 5.8; the critical path is 20 days (1 + 8 + 9 + 2). The identification of the critical path is an important feature of the planning process. Any delay in carrying out an activity on the critical path will inevitably delay project completion. On the other hand, activities that are not on the critical path can offer opportunities for some flexibility, because they may be able to be shifted to an earlier or later time slot to make optimal use of resources, without affecting the project completion date. This flexibility is referred to in terms of *float* but we shall return to discuss this aspect later.

The AoA approach to project planning is the approach used in the methods sometimes referred to as *Critical Path Analysis* or *Program Evaluation and Review Technique*, (PERT).

Activity on Node

In an AoN network each node represents an activity. Activities (nodes) are joined together with arrows, these indicating the direction of flow between activities. Figure 5.9 shows an AoN diagram consisting of two activities A and B with the arrow indicating that when A is completed then B can start. AoN nodes are usually rectangular and larger than AoA nodes, because the information relating to activities is inserted into the node area.

Figure 5.9 *AoN representation of project activities*

Figure 5.10 demonstrates some different dependencies. Activity C is dependent on Activity A only, whilst Activity D is dependent on both A and B.

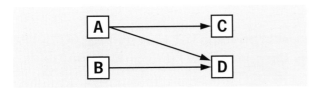

Figure 5.10 *AoN activity dependencies*

In AoN diagrams arrows are shown so that they do not cross each other. Dummy activities are *not* required in AoN networks to complete the logic.

One common convention in AoN is to show both a dependency time and an activity duration time. The dependency time is the time that must elapse between starting one activity and starting its dependent or following activity. The dependency time is shown under the arrow linking the activities. The activity's duration time is shown alongside or inside the node box as shown in Figure 5.11.

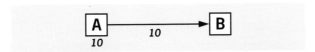

Figure 5.11 *Representing activity duration and activity dependency time in AoN diagrams*

In Figure 5.11, B can't start until A is finished. Therefore, the time taken to complete A is exactly the same as the dependency time. However, there could be situations where Activity B could start partway through Activity A's duration – say 3 days after A has started; the dependency time will reflect this. This is shown in Figure 5.12.

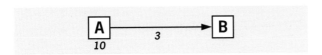

Figure 5.12 *Example of time overlap of two activities in AoN diagrams*

In both AoA and AoN networks, activities that are not linked by a dependency relationship could be allowed to occur simultaneously subject to the constraints imposed by other activities.

In Figure 5.13,

♦ E is dependent upon C and D. E can't start before C is finished but can begin halfway through D

♦ F and G depend upon E, but can both start before E finishes.

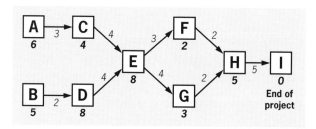

Figure 5.13 *AoN network*

If no dependency times are separately shown then you should assume that they are in all cases equal to the activity times.

Finally Figure 5.14 represents the same activities as Figure 5.8 showed in AoA form, but this time in AoN form.

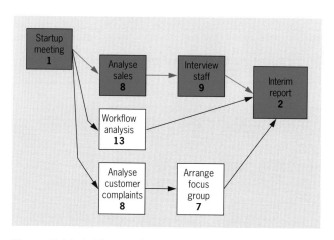

Figure 5.14 *AoN network for selected activities in project 'improve delivery times'*

This would be a good time to work through Activity 5.7

The concept of critical path is valid whatever the mode of representation. Again, any delay in activities on the critical path will cause a delay in project completion.

Activity 5.7 includes examples of network diagrams for a slightly more extensive project. You can use Activity 5.7 to test your network diagramming skills.

Float in network activities

Those activities that are not included in a network diagram's critical path may allow some flexibility in their scheduling.

After a network diagram has been created, a forward pass through the activities on each path from project start to project finish will allow the earliest start times for each activity to be established. A reverse pass from finish to start will allow the latest allowable start times for each activity to be deduced. For some activities these times will not be the same. Activities that can be carried out within a time window greater than their durations are said to have *float*. Float is the excess time available over an activity's estimated duration.

Float can be associated with a path from project start to finish. In general, if one activity doesn't use the float available to it, a succeeding activity might. Float which can be shared in this way is referred to as *path float* or *total float*. On the other hand, an activity could have a float available to it which could be used without having any effect on following activities. This can occur when a following activity can only be started at a time controlled by some other parallel activity. This type of float is termed *free float* because it is not shared along the path.

One issue that often arises in project work is the danger of overloading a resource. Float allows some choice over whether an activity is started at its earliest possible time or its latest possible time or somewhere in between. The flexibility can be used to reduce or avoid resource overloading.

Network diagrams are the key to successful understanding of relationships between activities and hence to the optimal planning of activities. A wide range of computer applications are available to help create network diagrams and project schedules and also different forms of reports, including resource allocation and project costs. Software choice may vary depending upon project size and complexity. You will be better placed to make intelligent use of such project management applications after having mastered the underlying concepts and application of network diagrams.

> **This would be a good time to work through Activity 5.8**

Network diagrams are powerful diagnostic tools, though they can become quite complex. Gantt charts are also widely used in project work and provide a relatively digestible view of a project plan.

What is a Gantt chart?

A Gantt chart is especially useful for presenting scheduling information to project stakeholders because it provides an at-a-glance summary of the project plan. In its simplest form a Gantt chart is often referred to as a bar chart and provides a view of things to be done against time. The things to be done can be at a high level – for instance project phases – or at any lower level in the WBS, for example, showing the scheduling details of activities within a single phase of a project, or it may show all the activities needing to be carried out in the entire project but this may be impractical in a single view for large or complex projects. Figure 5.15 is an example relating to one of the phases within the project *Improve Delivery Times*.

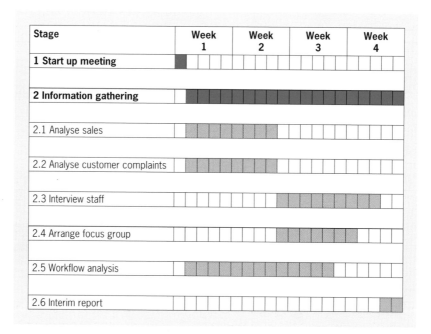

Figure 5.15 *Gantt chart for phase of project 'improve delivery times'*

The horizontal axis indicates the lapsed time indicated, for example, in week numbers or calendar dates. The length of time allocated to each activity is then represented as a bar extending over the corresponding time period.

Though simple, Gantt charts have an immediate impact. They are a powerful way of showing the length of time that different activities are expected to take, and which activities will be running at the same time. Examining a Gantt chart should allow you to consider whether:

◆ Any overlaps in project activities will overburden available resources. If the project team is small and one person in it is carrying out a number of activities, some revision of start and end dates may be needed. For example, in Figure 5.15, if the same person or people are involved in activities 2.1, 2.2 and 2.3 then resource problems may arise at the end of week 2 that could delay the project. Options may be to postpone the focus group or to seek additional resources.

◆ There are any opportunities to move activities to any periods when there is relatively low project activity. Some activity durations may include necessary waiting periods where resources may be under used. For example, an activity involving waiting for the return of questionnaires may allow other activities to be started earlier if this had the benefit of balancing the use of scarce resources over the project duration.

Any modifications to scheduling should be negotiated with those who have responsibility for specific activities. Additional considerations, such as staff leave or other staff or other resource commitments need to be taken into account during scheduling of project activities.

A Gantt chart commonly includes additional information. For example, project milestones representing key objectives and project deliverables may be highlighted. A simple Gantt chart can be further improved by indicating the dependencies of activities.

143

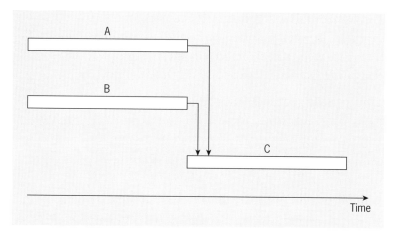

Figure 5.16 *Indicating activity dependencies in Gantt charts*

Figure 5.16 shows part of a Gantt chart in which arrows are included to indicate where dependency exists between activities. In the example shown, activities A and B are independent of each other but Activity C can only be started when both activities A and B have been completed. The dependency of Activities A to C can be described as 'finish to start'. This is also true for Activities B to C. When project management software is being used such arrows may be automatically added to Gantt chart representations and this greatly enhances the information available.

> **This would be a good time to work through Activity 5.9**

Taking stock

The detailed planning described in this chapter should complete a range of documentation that will provide a good basis for a project to be taken forward through its implementation stage. The documents and information that should now be available include:

- details of the project team, customer, sponsor and other stakeholders
- a vision statement and key objectives
- scope, constraints and deliverables

- risk analysis
- WBS and activity definition
- resource plan and commitment matrix
- a project budget
- network diagrams (AoA or AoN)
- critical path analysis
- Gantt chart.

Careful project planning and documentation is crucial to a successful project outcome. The planning processes that we have described when completed to the necessary level of detail will provide a project's baseline documentation. Changes inevitably occur as project implementation proceeds, but any changes must be negotiated and agreed between all parties affected. By managing against baseline documentation plus authorised changes, a project can remain under control. All changes that are subsequently necessary must, in addition to being agreed and approved, also be logged so that changes can be tracked and audited. Should a project fail the project documentation may need to withstand a legal challenge.5 Project planning

Activity 5.1
Team role types

Aim of this activity

- To identify the kind of role that you are most comfortable with in a team environment.

Useful resources for this activity

- *Change, Strategy and Projects at Work*
- Discussions with colleagues.

Background

This worksheet draws on the team roles explored in the book Successful Team Building, by Davis et al. (1992).* These team roles are driver, planner, enabler, executive and controller. Each of these main roles includes a subset of roles and attributes which are identified later.

Complete the questionnaire below. It consists of nine groups of statements with five statements in each group. You have 15 points to allocate to each group, and you should allocate points to each statement depending on how strongly you agree with them. For example, if you agree quite strongly with statement 2: 'I am systematic', you might want to give this five points or more, but might only want to award two points to statement 3: 'I can usually lay my hands on resources'. If you completely disagree with a statement, you needn't give it any points. However each group should total 15 points.

Try to do this without any preconception of the 'right' answers, but apportion the points to statements within groups to reflect an honest and critical self assessment. It may help you to think about past experiences that could justify your own view in each case.

I make a valuable member of any group because...

1   I am able to see opportunities for group development, and assign responsibilities to group members – without being too domineering

2   I am systematic in my analysis of the group's goals, and can devise plans to help the group achieve them

3   I can usually lay my hands on the resources the group needs to do this job

4   If I'm given a clear objective, I can be relied on to get on with the job

5   I can spot problems as they arise and show the group how to get back on track.

Total   15

---

* Davis, J., Milburn, P., Murphy, T. and Woodhouse, M. (1992). *Successful Team Building*, Kogan Page.

I would usually be invited to join a group because…

6   I'm good at checking the methods the group uses, and make sure there are procedures covering all major activities

7   I can be relied on to be strong and give direction to other team members

8   I can estimate rapidly what resources the team needs – and what they will cost

9   I can spot good ideas quickly – and get the rest of the group enthused about them

10 I'm good at giving the day-to-day guidance that results in smooth workflow and good working practices.

Total   15

I feel most satisfied when…

11 Promoting good teamwork and helping the team to work better together

12 Carefully analysing situations, weighing the evidence and drawing conclusions

13 Engaged in work that stretches my creativity and allows full flight to my imagination

14 Using tried and tested methods to produce new output

15 Working out a deal face-to-face with people who may have something new to offer.

Total   15

When my team is to work on a specific project…

16 My ability to get the right resources to the right place at the right time eliminates delays

17 My ability to follow instructions and get through the work assigned to me gives the group a fair chance of producing what is needed

18 My vigilance helps the team to identify and hopefully overcome barriers to high achievement

19 My ability to keep the team focused on its goals makes sure it delivers what is expected

20 My care in analysing the goals prevents us missing out activities and procedures.

Total   15

If I were to congratulate myself at the end of a project it would most likely be because…

21 My ability to budget for the project had ensured efficient use of resources

22 My ability to whip up enthusiasm for the project meant that the team cared about the result

23 My ability to structure tasks and organise the work flow kept the group highly productive

24   My ability to identify areas of greatest risk showed the team the best opportunities for improvements

25   My capacity for valid judgement gave the team someone to rely on to make major decisions and give clear direction.

	Total	15

My major contribution to teamwork is...

26   Having good ideas and coming up with novel ways of solving the group's problems

27   Working out the best way of organising the work to minimise wasted effort

28   Getting people to agree on actions that leave everyone satisfied

29   Quickly sensing when people are tense or stressed, and helping them to talk through their problem

30   Feeding back to the group information about the extent to which it is achieving, or has achieved, its goals.

	Total	15

If asked which part of the work gives me most satisfaction, I would say that I most enjoy...

31   Observing the group, keeping them on course and performing well

32   Deciding how the group should develop and making sure it does

33   Analysing goals, assessing risks and choosing the best course of action

34   Making sure that the group has the best materials and equipment with which to produce its output

35   Doing something that is neither too difficult, nor too easy, but which gives me a sense of achievement.

	Total	15

I would describe myself as someone who most of the time...

36   Enjoys working with the group to find practical solutions to operational problems

37   Enjoys work that enables me to satisfy my inquiring, investigative nature

38   Likes to exert strong influence on the group's decisions

39   Enjoys work that demands a systematic and thorough approach

40   Enjoys selling ideas, services or products.

	Total	15

I'm welcome in group problem-solving sessions because of my ability to ...

41 Give and take in my dealings with other team members, though I will try to persuade them to my point of view

42 Maintain a working environment in which the group can freely and openly discuss their views

43 Question the effectiveness and efficiency of each element of the team's activity to identify the real problems and their causes

44 Bring a degree of ingenuity and creativity to group problem solving

45 Fix the agenda and timetable for the activity.

Total 15

Scoring

Enter the score you gave for each statement against each statement number in the following grid.

1	7	13	2	8
19	25	26	20	21
32	38	44	33	39
Characteristic	Characteristic	Characteristic	Characteristic	Characteristic
A	B	C	D	E

14	3	9	15	4
27	16	22	28	17
45	34	40	41	35
Characteristic	Characteristic	Characteristic	Characteristic	Characteristic
F	G	H	I	J

10	11	5	6	12
23	29	18	24	30
36	42	31	37	43
Characteristic	Characteristic	Characteristic	Characteristic	Characteristic
K	L	M	N	0

Your scores should show as three entries in each block column. Add the totals of each column, and write these in the box titled A, B, etc. This gives you your preference score for each of the characteristics, which point towards preferred team roles.

Now transfer each characteristic total to the role boxes that follow. For example, totals A, B and C in the Driver category, totals D, E and F in the Planner category, and so on. (N.B. no characteristic should total more than 15 points.) Add the values together within each category to get your role scores.

When you have worked out all the role totals, check that they add up to 135.

The highest score is your primary preferred role, the next highest your secondary role. Do you have a third role, that scores more than 30? It is more likely that you only show the occasional high characteristic score in other roles.

Example		
A: Developer 11	A: Developer	D: Strategist
B: Director 9	B: Director	E: Estimator
C: Innovator 12	C: Innovator	F: Scheduler
DRIVER 32	DRIVER	PLANNER
G: Resource manager	J: Producer	M: Monitor
H: Promoter	K: Co-ordinator	N: Auditor
I: Negotiator	L: Maintainer	O: Evaluator
ENABLER	EXECUTIVE	CONTROLLER

Source: *Davies et al. (1992)*

This is what they all mean

Driver

A Driver is an intuitive decision maker, who uses instinct rather than analysis. Forward-looking, a risk taker and someone who loves change and life in the fast lane, the Driver is more interested in the big picture than the detail, and prefers to tell than sell. Drivers are enthusiastic organisers and team developers.

Within the Driver group, the Developer will identify directions for the team, clarify opportunities, ensure that the team grows along lines that suit it best, and builds the team's power and influence. The Director is dissatisfied with the way things are, and sees improvement as a challenge. Directors get things done – usually by others. They originate action, and will demand, instruct or coerce to get what they want done. The Innovator is the cornerstone of the team's creative effort. Imaginative and ingenious, the Innovator acts as the catalyst for the team, setting the team's sights on new opportunities and introducing new methods to improve the probability of the team's success.

Planner

A Planner is a logical thinker, who will analyse in depth, diagnose in detail and judge with confidence. They will take the Driver's 'required' future and interpret it in a way that the team can understand and use. Planners are organised and orderly, comfortable with regular procedures and conservative in their approach to change. They are forward-looking, and good at setting targets. They set high standards for themselves and others.

Within the Planner group, the Strategist can take a loosely defined aim and develop it into a detailed strategic statement. They can visualise the organisation needed to achieve the aim, how to build it and the effect it will have on the people involved. They can link what has gone before with the future and see what might go wrong. The Estimator assesses how much work the team is capable of doing, and by interpreting the strategy, judges what capacity is likely to be required. They will analyse the strategic goals in order to determine what resources the team will need. The Scheduler analyses the tasks to be performed by the team, and works out which tasks are best suited to each role, which activities to combine, and which must be performed in sequence or in parallel. They determine what resources are needed and when and where they are required.

Enabler

Enablers rely on their personal values to direct their decisions. They are natural sales people, and work to convert people to their point of view. Outgoing and persuasive, they are enthusiastic for anything new. They are not always well organised, but they will take on a plan and make sure that the team gets the resources it needs to follow it through.

Within the Enabler group, the Resource Manager understands the nature of the resources needed by the team and how they should be used and controlled. They are best at identifying the resources the team will need for its future activities, noting any problems and updating the Planner. The Resource Manager is the person who will consider the personal development of team members and identify appropriate training. The Promoter will publicise the team's successes, selling the team to everyone outside, and selling the plans and the future to team members. The Promoter will also highlight goals and strategies, raise team enthusiasm and work to overcome resistance to change. The Negotiator gives the team a realistic view of the outside world. They have a clear picture of the people with whom the team must negotiate; people who can either help or block progress. The Negotiator will identify what people expect from the team and how satisfied they are, and will make proposals for improvements to the team output and bargain for team resources.

Executive

If you are an Executive, you will base decisions on observation and how you feel about what you see. They are realists – there is a job that needs doing, so they do it. They are capable of turning instruction into action, systematically, patiently and completely. They live in the present and are not too worried about what the future might bring. The Executive will make great efforts to ensure that the team works in harmony to get things done.

Within the Executive group, the Producer puts plans and instructions into action. These are the goal setters and goal achievers, but they are also realists – they don't try to achieve the impossible. Producers need a system or procedures to follow (creating their own if necessary), and will participate in job design and organising workflow. The Co-ordinator is best at balancing the varied and conflicting demands placed on the team by different parts of the organisation, and makes sure that each team member has their fair share of day-to-day work and individual tasks. They will develop and regulate the team's standards of behaviour, and will organise individuals into a working team. The Maintainer is the person who holds the team together. Natural counsellors, they can spot conflict early on, and help those involved to resolve the issues. They can help all team members to set realistic goals and workable strategies, and give continual support to the group.

Controller

The Controller is an analytical thinker, who will base their decisions on an analysis of what happened in the past. Controllers enjoy developing a detailed understanding of the way the team works, the systems it uses, the progress it is making and the results it has achieved. They use their experience and knowledge to give advice and guidance on target setting and the solution of problems, and can assess in detail the costs incurred by the team's operations and the benefits achieved by it.

In the Controller group, the Auditor will analyse the team's activities in detail. They will check that resources are of adequate quality to match the activity, and will check for errors and their cause. The Monitor will produce the team's formal records. They will observe the team in operation, in the work it does and as a group working together, to ensure that the team is following procedures, and will provide feedback on this to the Planner. Monitors are the progress chasers. The Evaluator is the team's judge or quality manager, able to assess in detail the costs and benefits of the team's operation. The Evaluator will report whether the team has provided what was asked for, when needed, to the right standard, and at cost within budget.

Discussion

You may have found that you had a sharp profile with a clear preference in one or two roles. Alternatively you may have shown a broad profile across several or even all roles. There are no 'correct' answers for this assessment, because all roles can make important contributions. A team that does not collectively include a balance of preferred roles may be lacking in some of the attributes of missing or weakly represented roles and may not be as successful as it could be. Another point to note is that these preferred roles are not set in stone and can change over time and with exposure to different workplace environments.

Activity 5.2
Specialist requirements in project team for proposed project

Aim of this activity

◆ To review elements of specialist skills, knowledge or experience that would be needed in a project team assembled to plan and implement your proposed project.

Useful resources for this activity

◆ *Change, Strategy and Projects at Work*

◆ Resources at work

◆ Discussions with colleagues.

The nature of a project team can differ considerably depending, for example, upon the environment in which an organisation functions and the scale or complexity of project that is involved. For large scale projects a project team may be concerned primarily with delegating actions and then monitoring and controlling the progress made by others. By contrast for a small scale project a project team may consist of individuals with roles that are largely hands-on. If as the project lead you were able to select people to work on your team, a sensible approach would be to match the needs of the project from the available range of skills, team roles, knowledge and experience that each individual could contribute. If specialist skills, knowledge and experience were required then these may be available within certain job functions such as engineer, accountant, designer and so on. Here I am using the term 'specialist skills' to distinguish them from more general employability skills.

Complete the following table to identify any specialist skills, knowledge and experience in a project team assembled for your proposed project. Do not feel obliged to invent any needs where none exist; an object here is to highlight any implications for project team membership and costs, should an external specialist need to be bought in.

	Description of need	Covered by known individuals or functions	Covered by self	Covered by an external resource
Specialist skills/ knowledge?				
Experience level?				

Activity 5.3
WBS for creation of home office

Aims of this activity

◆ To identify the component activities of a WBS for a simple project

◆ To draw out a WBS hierarchy

◆ To create a WBS hierarchy for your proposed project.

Useful resources for this activity

◆ *Change, Strategy and Projects at Work*

◆ Discussions with colleagues

(a) Assume that you don't have a home office or the equipment needed in it, but that you do have a spare room suitable for developing as a home office. The office would require a reasonable standard of the usual computer and communication equipment, desk and filing cabinets and so on.

Now identify the component activities of a WBS that would describe the creation of such a home office. Where would you start? How many different stages would you envisage? Break down each stage (or task) into its constituent activities. Record your results in the following table, modifying it if required.

Notice that we have adopted the common convention of referencing the top level (which in this case is the project title, but could alternatively be the title of a portion of a larger project) and which I have denoted as a zero. Following this convention be careful to note that a three level hierarchy has two levels of work breakdown, a four level hierarchy has three levels of work breakdown, and so on.

Now use the table to create a three level hierarchical list for the home office project.

Title of project: 0. Create home office	
	Brief description of activity
Stage 0.1 Activity 0.1.1 Activity 0.1.2 Activity 0.1.3 ...	
Stage 0.2 Activity 0.2.1 Activity 0.2.2 Activity 0.2.3 ...	
Stage 0.3 Activity 0.3.1 Activity 0.3.2 Activity 0.3.3 ...	

After you have completed this, compare your WBS with ours towards the end of this activity.

(b) Sketch out a graphical representation of a project WBS hierarchy using your own answer to part (a) or using ours. You could alternatively investigate what options are available for using your computer to draw out a hierarchical diagram. The example of a WBS hierarchy in a graphical format that we present here was created using an organisational chart feature on a word processor application.

(c) After having completed parts (a) and (b) you should feel able to create a WBS hierarchy for your proposed project. You should attempt this now.

Discussion – Part (a)

Your answer may differ considerably depending upon your interpretation of what needs to be done. For a project in the workplace the WBS would be discussed and agreed by the project team. The WBS for this example is simple. A more extensive WBS could result from a more detailed exploration (and breakdown) of each activity and would depend upon the scale and complexity of the project.

Title of project: 0. Create home office	
	Stage/activity description
Stage 0.1	Identify requirements
Activity 0.1.1	Identify ICT needs
Activity 0.1.2	Identify required office furniture and fittings
Activity 0.1.3	Define layout
Stage 0.2	Purchase equipment, office furniture and fittings
Activity 0.2.1	Identify acceptable suppliers
Activity 0.2.2	Order items
Stage 0.3	Install facilities
Activity 0.3.1	Assemble and position office furniture and fittings
Activity 0.3.2	Position and install ICT equipment
Activity 0.3.3	Check for correct and convenient use

Discussion – Part (b)

In general you would need to present a WBS hierarchy to include all the significant activities that need to be identified, planned and budgeted. Large and complex projects may require many levels in their WBS hierarchy though a large WBS can be handled in manageable chunks rather than trying to represent the whole WBS in one diagram.

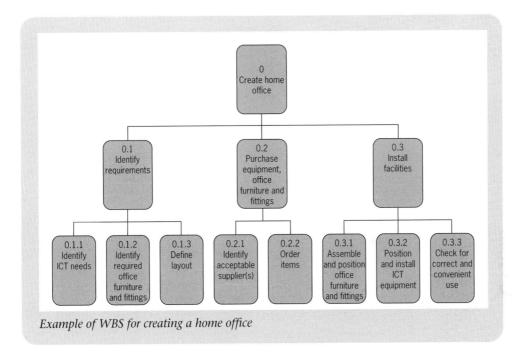

Example of WBS for creating a home office

Activity 5.4
Resourcing project activity

Aim of this activity

◆ To estimate the duration and resources needed by each activity in the lowest layer of a WBS list.

Useful resources for this activity

◆ *Change, Strategy and Projects at Work*

◆ Resources at work

◆ Discussions with colleagues.

Create a table similar to the one that follows suited to your proposed project's WBS. Then enter each of the lower level activities for your proposed project into the appropriate fields.

For each activity identify each type of resource needed (e.g., person, machine time, materials, office services and so on) and estimate the activity duration and the time that each resource is needed for. You need to do this before you can make a realistic estimate of the costs of each activity. Try to find out the cost associated with each resource that is needed and record this in the cost column. Remember that the time a resource is needed for may not necessarily be the same as the duration of the activity.

You will need to use your judgement over the sensible use of resources. For example, you may decide that one person can carry out a given activity, but if two suitable people were available this may decrease the time each person is required for, as well as the activity duration. This could be beneficial to the project, but not necessarily to your workplace if the same resources are likely to be needed in different areas at the same time.

Proposed project title: 0				
	Identify resources needed	Activity duration (units)	Time each resource is needed for (units)	Identified cost (units)
Stage 0.1				
Activity 0.1.1	(a) (b) (c)			
Activity 0.1.2	(a) (b) (c)			
Activity 0.1.3	(a) (b) ...			
Stage 0.2				
Activity 0.2.1	(a) ...			

Activity 5.5
Project cost estimate

Aim of this activity

◆ To prepare an improved project estimate.

Useful resources for this activity

◆ *Change, Strategy and Projects at Work*

◆ Resources at work

◆ Discussions with colleagues

You should use this activity to obtain an improved budget estimate for your proposed project. Again, you should seek advice from within your organisation (e.g., from your finance department) to learn about the approaches used for estimating project costs in areas such as staffing.

Having looked at the detailed WBS and the resources needed for your proposed project you should be in a better position to obtain an improved cost estimate for your project.

Return to Activity 5.4 to refer to costs you've already identified relating to specific project activities and use a table structure similar to that shown in Figure 5.3 to produce a budget estimate for your project. Alternatively, you could use a spreadsheet application for this purpose.

Discussion

An estimate of the project budget required will be an important feature of a business case for your proposed project. You should note how your project estimate has changed from your earlier estimate.

Activity 5.6
Commitment matrix

Aim of this activity

◆ To establish a commitment matrix for your proposed project.

Useful resources for this activity

◆ *Change, Strategy and Projects at Work*

◆ Resources at work

◆ Discussions with colleagues

◆ Previous activities relating to this chapter.

Before a project is to be implemented it is necessary to plan the allocation of particular resources to activities and identify the individuals responsible for each activity or group of activities.

Create an extended version of Table 5.2 to accommodate the WBS activities for your project. Use this to enter the required information for each activity.

You should ascertain for each activity who would be responsible, whether training is likely to be needed, what other facilities or resources would be required and so on. Remember that in Activities 5.4 and 5.5 you identified the resources required, so you will need to refer back to these.

Again, you should modify the layout of the commitment matrix to suit the needs of your proposed project.

Activity 5.7
Network diagrams

Aim of this activity

◆ To develop your skills in constructing project network diagrams.

Useful resources for this activity

◆ *Change, Strategy and Projects at Work*

The case study scenario is described in the box below. Read through the description given in the opening paragraphs then follow the activity list for the first phase of the project (1 to 8) relating to how each is shown in the two network diagrams that follow.

An hotel business centre

Background:

A group of small hotels attracts only a very general (and not very profitable) clientele and mostly at weekends. The evidence of this is that many rooms are not filled on weekdays.

The group's directors have agreed that they must make their hotels more attractive to business customers as this would be more profitable with steady demand for rooms on weekday nights.

Reception staff have pointed out that those business customers who do use their hotels are often frustrated that a comprehensive range of office facilities are not available for them to use during their stay. This is an important issue for business customers who may wish to access a computer with printer, a photocopier and other ICT equipment such as a paper-based facsimile machine. Although guest rooms are equipped with broadband lines and sockets (and of course telephones), this does not satisfy the wider needs of business users.

After some deliberation, the hotel management has decided to undertake the development of a 'business centre' at one of its hotels to attract business customers. They would be charged depending upon their use of services.

At an initial project team meeting ideas are discussed and a set of key activities needing to be undertaken are agreed. The following list refers to these activities (corresponding to the second level of the project work breakdown hierarchy). Each activity has been given a simple reference number rather than a hierarchical number to assist the clarity of the network diagrams and the duration of each activity in days is shown in parentheses. Some nominal activities having zero duration have been added to mark the start and end of the two phases of the project.

Activity list:

1. *Start (0)* (beginning of phase 1)
2. Market investigation (12)
3. Define customer wants (4)
4. Specify facilities (6)
5. Competitive tender (7)
6. Cost–benefit report (3)
7. Board scrutiny (3)
8. *Go-ahead decision (0)* (end of phase 1, beginning of phase 2)
9. Refurbish room (10)
10. Install furniture and fittings (5)
11. Install security (2)
12. Install ICT equipment (5)
13. Write training/user guide (4)
14. Train support staff (5)
15. Develop billing system (4)
16. Produce brochures (5)

17. Send out brochures (5)

18. Handover (0) (end of phase 2)

Notes on activities and constraints:

The following dependencies apply to the project activity list.

For activities in the first phase:

◆ after 1 is completed, 2 can start

◆ after 2 is completed, 3 can start

◆ after 3 is completed, both 4 and 6 can start (simultaneously)

◆ after 4 is completed, 5 can start

◆ after both 5 and 6 are completed, 7 can start

◆ after 7 is completed, 8 can start.

For activities in the second phase:

◆ following the go-ahead decision (activity 8) activities 9, 13, 15 and 16 can start immediately

◆ after 9 is completed, 10 and 11 can both start (simultaneously)

◆ after both 10 and 11 are completed, 12 can start

◆ after both 12 and 13 are completed, 14 can start

◆ after 16 is completed, 17 can start

◆ after 14, 15 and 17 are completed, 18 can start.

After familiarising yourself with the network diagrams for the first phase of this project, you should produce your own diagrams (both AoA and AoN) for the second phase. You should label each activity clearly in your diagrams to ensure good clarity and include the activity durations in your diagrams.

Our answer is shown at the end of this chapter's activities. When you have completed this activity, you should feel sufficiently confident in your use of network diagrams to create one for your own project.

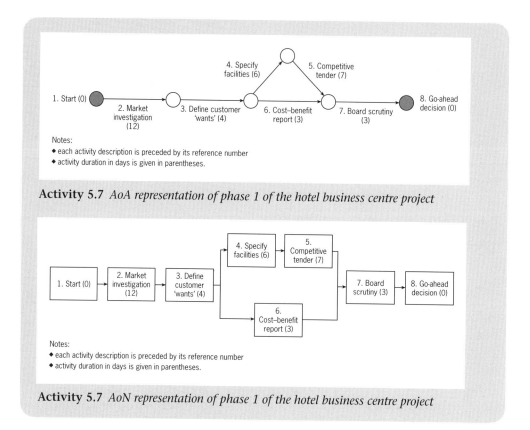

Activity 5.7 *AoA representation of phase 1 of the hotel business centre project*

Notes:
♦ each activity description is preceded by its reference number
♦ activity duration in days is given in parentheses.

Activity 5.7 *AoN representation of phase 1 of the hotel business centre project*

Activity 5.8
Network diagram for your work-based project

Aim of this activity

♦ To create a network diagram for your work-based project.

Useful resources for this activity

♦ *Change, Strategy and Projects at Work*

♦ Resources at work

♦ Discussions with colleagues.

Create a network diagram for your proposed project.

Discussion

Constructing a network diagram in itself should help you to clarify your planning. However, after you have completed this activity you may still feel that you have not defined the sequences of activities in your project entirely satisfactorily. In practice you could expect to modify your network diagram as your plans develop further or as circumstances change.

Activity 5.9
Gantt charts

Aims of this activity

◆ To use a Gantt chart to represent a project schedule

◆ To create a Gantt chart for your proposed project.

Useful resources for this activity

◆ *Change, Strategy and Projects at Work*

◆ Resources at work

◆ Discussions with colleagues.

(a) Sketch a Gantt chart for the case study (hotel business centre) in Activity 5.7. You should assume that all the activities start at the earliest possible time. I have used the term 'sketch' to suggest that you do this using pencil and paper. You may have access to project management software or various spreadsheets that can be modified to do this for you to a professional standard of presentation, but sketching out a Gantt chart should provide sufficient consolidation of your learning.

My sketch is given at the end of these activities.

(b) When you have completed part (a) you should feel confident about creating a Gantt chart for your proposed project. You should do this now.

Discussion: Activity 5.7

AoA and AoN network diagrams for the hotel business centre project are shown below.

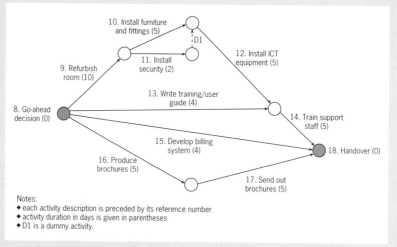

AoA representation of phase 2 of the hotel business centre project

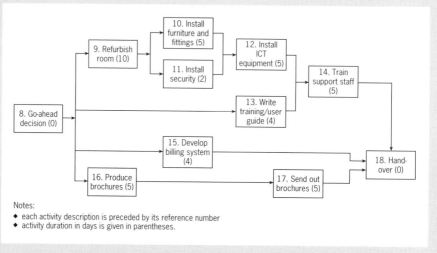

AoN representation of phase 2 of the hotel business centre project

Discussion: Activity 5.9

A 'sketched' Gantt chart for the hotel business centre project follows. I have used a diamond symbol to represent the activities that have zero duration. These are useful as project milestones, though the project start has no significance here in terms of any outcomes. Also shown is a view of a corresponding Gantt chart produced by a project management application.

Sketched Gantt chart for hotel business centre project

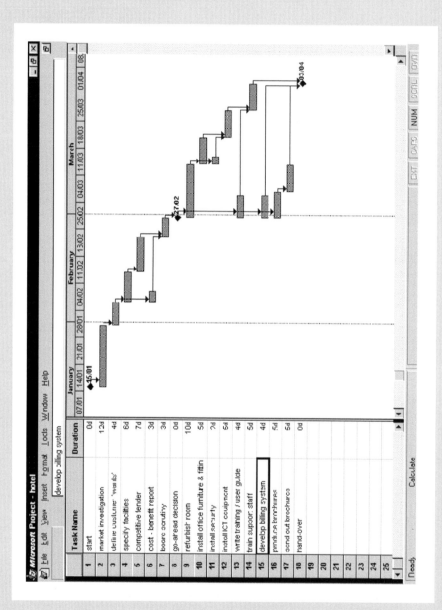

View of a Gantt chart for hotel business centre project using a project management software package

6 Project implementation

When all plans are finally authorised and the project is approved, the project implementation can commence at the date envisaged in the project schedule. It is usually a good idea to build in a start-up meeting to mark the start of the journey and to provide an opportunity for people who may not have worked together previously to meet.

Start-up meeting

A start-up meeting can fulfil a number of purposes:

◆ to present or reiterate the project vision and to enthuse project stakeholders

◆ to ensure that everybody involved knows exactly what the project entails, how it supports the organisation's strategy, what the project's objectives are and how the project team will achieve them

◆ to discuss the project activities, milestones, performance indicators, schedule and budget

◆ to give the team members an opportunity to ask questions, hear other people's questions, and clear up any doubts and queries

◆ to establish the procedures for communication and to disseminate contact details of everyone involved with the project

◆ to ensure people are clear about decision-making procedures, including limits on spending levels, reporting progress or flagging up problems, calling project meetings and so on

◆ finally, because a newly formed project team which has not previously worked together needs time to develop to optimum effectiveness, a start-up meeting is helpful and could usefully be supplemented with additional events to aid the team's development.

Making and monitoring progress

The purpose of the implementation phase is to create the reality from the project plans by systematically achieving each project objective and ultimately a successfully delivered project outcome that meets the specified time – cost – quality criteria. During this period frequent team meetings will be needed to report on and discuss progress achieved, the progress that yet needs to be made in following periods, the implications of unforeseen problems and options for their solution and any necessary changes to plans. The process is summarised in Figure 6.1.

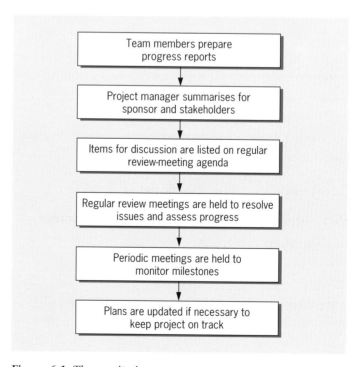

Figure 6.1 *The monitoring process*

Source: *Bruce and Langdon (2000)*

Reviewing and reporting progress

The achievement of a successful project outcome is dependent upon the monitoring and reporting of a whole range of things – progress against specific objectives, the rate at which resources are being consumed, how well the project team is working together, maintaining close contact between the project team, project sponsor, project customer and other project stakeholders and so on. These are all prerequisites necessary for developing and communicating a realistic view of project progress against plan at any particular time. Effective information flows to and from the project team will enable plans to be reviewed, problems to be discussed and effective and timely evasive or corrective action to be taken where needed. The key to all this is effective and regular communication.

Summarising the basis for effective communication and review

♦ Frequent and regular team review meetings with clear and consistent agenda, promptly circulated meeting notes which include specific action points agreed and carried out.

♦ Working sub-group meetings, where appropriate, to thrash out questions of specific detail.

♦ Short, regular progress reports to a project's sponsor, customer and other stakeholders.

♦ Actively managed stakeholder relationships – identifying those whose support for the project is critical and those who may hinder project progress.

♦ Use of informal as well as formal communication channels to build supporting project-related 'intelligence'.

> ◆ Encouragement of frank, honest, but objective reporting with focus on solutions rather than blame when things go wrong.
>
> ◆ Support and feedback to project team members to maintain motivation and commitment.

In some organisations face to face meetings may be a rare luxury, especially where normal job functions (or the project itself) require team members to work in multiple locations and perhaps in different countries. However, modern communication technologies help compensate for any limitations in the frequency of face-to-face meetings. Examples are video conferencing, web meeting applications and mobile applications that can substitute for real meetings and the use of project websites and project blogs and mobile data technologies to ensure up-to-date information is readily available to all who need access to it.

Monitoring progress against plan

As a result of the planning and costing carried out prior to project implementation, a project leader will be aware of the total expenditure to be committed over the duration of the project. This can be plotted as a graph of the planned expenditure to be committed (or budgeted cost) against elapsed time as shown in Figure 6.2. The expenditure to be committed generally increases slowly at first, then more rapidly towards the middle period of the project, before rising more slowly towards the total estimated project at project completion. The plot often resembles a shallow 'S' shape; hence it is called an 'S-curve'.

If a project S-curve is to be used as a gauge of project progress there are dangers that it could be misinterpreted, leading to an unjustifiably pessimistic or optimistic conclusion. For example a lower expenditure than planned for a particular stage of the project could mean that cost savings had been achieved, but it would be more likely that some activities and the expenditure associated with them had been delayed.

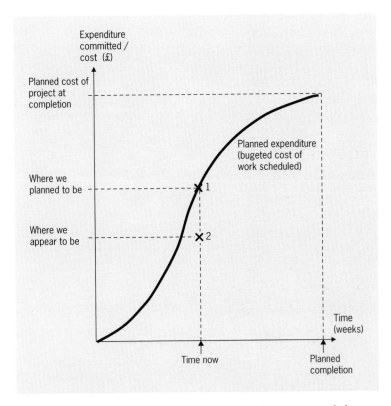

Figure 6.2 *The progress dilemma: At 'time now' our costs are below budget, but is progress to plan?*

This judgement could be a real dilemma for a project leader and the project team.

A more objective assessment of progress can be made using the 'earned-value' approach which is depicted in Figure 6.3. In this approach the progress of the project in monetary terms is reviewed in terms of the work that has actually been completed to the review point.

Three curves are used to carry out this assessment:

◆ The budgeted cost for the work scheduled; this indicates what the monetary cost (or value) of the work scheduled (or planned) should be at any time.

◆ The budgeted cost of the work performed (actually achieved); this indicates what the cost should be for the work carried out to the review point.

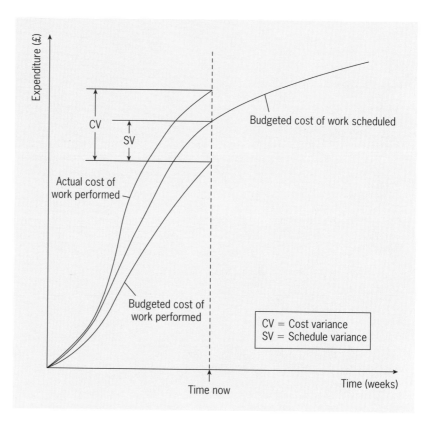

Figure 6.3 *Earned-value monitoring of project progress*

♦ The actual cost of the work performed; this indicates the real cost or earned value of the work carried out to the review point.

This method is dependent upon the 'costs' referred to above as representing value. This may be straight forward where, for instance, attainment of project milestones leads to staged payments, but for an internal project the 'costs' will need to reflect the value of progress made towards the final service or product outcomes that the project is designed to achieve.

Two important indicators of progress result from this approach. The cost variance is an indicator of how the cost committed varies from that planned for the progress achieved to date whilst the schedule variance is an indicator of how the timing of the project activities varies from that planned.

Using this approach a more robust assessment can be made of what has really been achieved to date. A forward projection can then be made to estimate any changes to the project's likely final cost and completion date.

Factors that can change projects

In turbulent global conditions, a change programme and the projects cascading from it can be overtaken by events. In these circumstances more frequent periodic reviews and revisions are likely to be needed. Additional factors that may need a project's current plans to be amended can be identified by asking questions such as:

◆ Is the business case for the project still valid?

◆ Has the project customer changed their requirements?

◆ Is the project meeting its objectives?

◆ Have any better ways of meeting project objectives been identified?

◆ What changes to project risks have been identified?

◆ What changes to resource needs have been identified?

◆ Should the project proceed to the next stage or phase?

It is generally necessary to accept that change within projects will occur, particularly if they are highly innovative or extend over a lengthy period of time. For example, if a customer's needs change then this is likely to be reflected in the need to modify a project's outcome and this may have implications for individual project objectives, the scheduling of work and the acceptance criteria used at handover to confirm the quality and function of project outcomes.

Another example of change arising during implementation is as a result of scope creep. Often innovative insights may lead to the 'enhancement' of an original project specification, but such enhancements may incur additional cost or delay and may not necessarily be valued as 'enhancement' by the project customer. Examples of other factors that can have significant impact on project plans during implementation include organisational restructuring, changes in staff roles or the departure of key members of a project team.

Not all causes of project change during implementation are bad. For instance it may be necessary to revise a project timetable because a milestone has been reached more quickly than expected, or a customer sees wider implications for the outcomes of a project, perhaps in terms of a new market opening for example. Such events may lead to requests for an extension of the work being carried out.

In some circumstances, plans may be seen only as indicators of the original thinking. It may be expected that as a project progresses, new insights will lead to the revision of the original plans. A 'sliding window' approach to project planning focuses only on the detailed planning of the next stages and acknowledges that accurate and detailed planning of later stages is unrealistic in the context of a rapidly changing environment. In some circumstances, a preoccupation with defining details of work that cannot reasonably be defined yet, may be considered wasteful of resources. This approach may involve a higher degree of risk and uncertainty reflecting the emergent processes associated with some change situations.

Where project specifications and plans are changed as discussed previously the process must be subject to the process of change control. Change control refers to the process of clearly identifying, recording and communicating changes to a project's specification and documentation. Systematic change control procedures are required to ensure that all project stakeholders use a project's current working documents rather than ones that have been made obsolete by changes to specification or procedures. An alternative term *change management* is also used to describe the same process, but this can create confusion in relation to the wider context of managing change described in the early chapters of this book.

Project implementation is likely to be characterised by periods of good progress and periods when progress slows as unforeseen problems surface. Dealing with problems effectively is an essential part of making progress at all levels of change or project implementation but there are many tools and techniques available to help.

Problem identification

An experienced project team provided with accurate and timely information may be able to see potential problems developing and overcome them before they cause major disruption to progress. A useful algorithm for the effective management of problems is to:

◆ agree what the problem is

◆ identify the possible causes

◆ generate options for resolving the problem

◆ assess the options and select an appropriate one

◆ implement the selected solution

◆ review the result.

Problem-solving techniques

Table 6.1 presents a selection of techniques commonly applied to a variety of problem-solving situations. Each of these is presented in more detail in Appendix: *Techniques for problem solving and decision making*, along with brief notes to explain each technique's use. You may come across variations on these techniques and in the way they are applied. You may find that some of the techniques described in the appendix use components of accompanying techniques, for example, brain storming features in more than one of the described techniques.

This would be a good time to work through Activity 6.1

Table 6.1 *Some decision-making/problem-solving techniques*

Technique	Description
1 Brainstorming	Freethinking contributions from all group members in a non-judgemental, non-threatening environment.
2 Ishikawa/fishbone diagram	Technique systematically investigates the root causes of problems from a knowledge of the symptoms, prior to proposing a solution.
3 Nominal group technique	A formal approach to problem solving which involves contributions from all members of a group and uses consensus to evaluate and rank all the ideas generated.
4 Six thinking hats technique	The structure of a group meeting is referenced to an imaginary hat colour, the colour indicating which mode of thinking is currently engaged. For example, during red hat thinking it is allowable for people to express feelings and frustrations.
5 Plan–Do–Check–Act or PDCA cycle	Cyclic approach to investigating possible solutions for process improvement in a minimally disruptive way.
6 Paired comparisons	Method for producing a ranked list of options based upon systematically comparing pairs of options.
7 Comparison tables	Comparison tables may be used to compare a limited number of options using weightings to express the importance of perceived benefits or attributes.
8 Pareto analysis	A Pareto analysis identifies those problem areas that when solved will result in the greatest improvement or benefit.
9 Decision-tree analysis	Use of decision trees to analyse possible decision options and consequential events expressed in terms of probability.

Activity 6.1
Problem-solving techniques

Aim of this activity

♦ To reinforce your knowledge of problem-solving techniques by relating them to your past and/or current experience at work.

Useful resources for this activity

♦ *Change, Strategy and Projects at Work*

◆ Resources at work

◆ Discussions with colleagues.

On page 179 of *Change, Strategy and Projects at Work*, we note that problem solving involves:

◆ agreeing what the problem is

◆ identifying the possible causes

◆ generating options for resolving the problem

◆ assessing the options and select an appropriate one

◆ implementing the selected solution

◆ reviewing the result.

Think about a past or current problem that you have experienced/ are experiencing at work and complete the table below.

◆ What is/was the problem?

◆ What are/were the possible causes identified?

◆ What options were/have been generated for resolving the problem?

◆ How did you/will you assess the options and select an appropriate one?

◆ How did you/will you implement the selected solution?

◆ How did you/will you review the result?

◆ Was the problem solved? If not, why not? What further action did you take?

◆ Did you/will you use any problem-solving techniques, including those mentioned in Table 6.1 of *Change, Strategy and Projects at Work*? If so, which ones did/ will you use and why? Did you find the technique (s) helpful? If yes, why? If no, why not?

Discussion

In any project you're almost certainly going to come across problems at some stage, so it useful to have an awareness of a variety of techniques to help you to solve them. Your choice of technique(s) will depend on the nature and complexity of the problem; however, whichever techniques you employ, it is vital to make sure that you spend enough time making sure (as far as is possible) that you have identified the problem and its causes correctly. The most common cause of failure to solve a problem is incorrect identification in the first place – thus leading to wasted time and effort in solving the 'wrong' problem.

7 Project closure and evaluation

Project closure and evaluation

From the moment a project is handed over successfully to a satisfied, even delighted, project customer there may seem to be little further that needs to be done within the project lifecycle. There may also be pressure to move on to new work or additional projects. However, a project initiative usually represents a considerable investment of time, money and human resources and importantly, a significant learning opportunity. A conscious effort is required to ensure that organisational and personal learning is maximised and recorded so that lessons learned are not lost, but secured for future reference.

At project closure the following actions, as a minimum, need to be taken:

◆ Orderly and secure archival of project data, specifications, meeting notes, records of problem solving processes and so on.

◆ Project report.

◆ Project evaluation/debriefing meeting.

Project-related information

A project will generate information that may be potentially useful for future projects within the organisation, for example:

◆ Project planning data: various versions of project plans, contacts data, meeting notes and agendas and action checklists, key communications in the form of letters, emails and other forms, project deliverables in the form of documentation and project reports.

183

♦ Information relating, for example, to market studies, analyses and assessments by team members and others, problem-solving events and solutions adopted, proposed new business models and industry benchmarks.

The effective archiving of data and materials requires that someone should be responsible for bringing together all project data in whatever form is necessary (electronic or hard copy) to conform with organisational policy. Various groupings of documents within folders may need to be accompanied by summaries or contents lists. An appropriate indexing system should allow required documents to be found without difficulty.

The form of electronic data storage should ensure it's availability and accessibility for the foreseeable future (however that may be defined), bearing in mind how some storage technologies are subject to rapid changes. Projects are likely to include information and data which could be useful to non-legitimate parties such as business competitors, so appropriate secure, controlled and logged access to project data may be necessary.

Some projects produce artefacts other than documentation or software; for example, prototype models and demonstrator equipment. These may also need storing, destroying or delivering to the project customer, subject to what may have already been agreed.

There is another reason why project documentation and artefacts should be properly archived. Unfortunately, despite initially accepting a project hand-over, a project customer, (particularly an external one) may at some point, claim that a particular feature of the delivered project is unsatisfactory. Having access to project records can be crucial where some aspect of the specified project outcome or some change to specification is disputed. If a dispute turns into litigation then project records may become legal evidence. Poorly kept or incomplete records may leave the organisation with a weak defence against a claim.

Project reports

Reports may already have been written as specific items of project deliverables as well as for other reasons, for example, reports to a project team or project sponsor. Again, it is important that project information and experiences, whether good or bad, are recorded for organisational purposes. Project reports can bring together otherwise disparate pieces of information, for example, providing an overview explanation of what happened and why certain decisions were taken. A project report written primarily as a closure document for internal use should place on record what has actually been done and achieved and reference all matters of potential value to the organisation arising from the project experience, providing links to the project archive where related details and documentation can be accessed.

The style and structure of project reports can vary widely depending upon what they are going to be used for and whether they are produced primarily for internal or external use. An external customer may prescribe the form of report that is required; perhaps a very formal collection of facts with little narrative about process, or alternatively a less formal report with greater emphasis on explanation about how the project developed.

If a project was set up to investigate a particular problem, a suitable structure may follow the lines of:

◆ Executive summary – a summary highlighting the main points and recommendations

◆ Introduction – an explanation of the problem and the background to the project

◆ Methodology – techniques for gathering then analysing relevant data

◆ Findings – key issues emerging from the data gathered, and options for their resolution

◆ Recommendations – the next steps

◆ Appendices – for example, project personnel, staff interviewed, copy of questionnaire used, Gantt chart and other supporting documentation.

Alternative report structures could be based upon the chronological stages that a project passed through, or upon a department-by-department contribution to project activities. A closure report written primarily for the originating organisation's use should include sections that capture a reflective evaluation and the organisational learning resulting from the project experiences. These are the main outcomes of a project debriefing process.

Project debrief and learning

> **Those who cannot remember their past are condemned to repeat it.**
>
> **George Santayana**

A project debrief is a meeting which provides an opportunity to revisit and learn from the project experience in its entirety. It should occur within a reasonable time of project closure. This helps to ensure that as many of the original project team members as possible can attend, bearing in mind that following project completion other activities will compete for their time. Stakeholder attendance may be limited to internal stakeholders, but depending upon the level of partnership and co-operation, external project customers and consultants may also be included.

A debrief meeting is intended to capture learning from a completed project, so it is important to encourage a more reflective stance than may have been possible at project team meetings. The emphasis of a debrief meeting is to focus on lessons that can be learned from the project experience, both what went well and problems that arose. This is best achieved in an atmosphere characterised by a degree of humility and honesty where questions of blame are decidedly off-limit.

At the conclusion of a project, questions such as the ones that follow will help stimulate a reflective perspective:

- Has the project met all of its objectives within the constraints of time, cost and quality? What variances arose?

- Did objectives or constraints change during the project? If so, were these agreed as a result of changes to the specification of project outcomes or because of difficulties in managing resources?

- What actions were taken to reverse any negative trends or to maintain positive ones?

- What are the specific results and benefits? How do these compare with those originally planned (the baseline plan)?

- Has everything been achieved that should have been achieved? If not, are the reasons clearly understood and documented?

- What, if any, risks materialised during project implementation? Was the risk assessment realistic in retrospect?

- Have all costs been accounted for? Did any significant cost arise that were not anticipated at the start?

- Have all project-specific resources been accounted for and where appropriate, re-assigned?

- Are there any outstanding issues needing resolution?

- Overall what other aspects went well and what others didn't?

- Has all learning been recorded for future use?

A project will have generated a lot of information and experiences that may be of value to other projects or as part of individual and group learning. Some of this information may not be recorded in normal project reports, but putting it into a form where others can access it can save much time on other projects. Such information may also be valuable as benchmarks against which future work can be measured.

There is a danger that all information, however trivial or fragmented may be stored en-mass rather than sifted and sorted. However, taking the trouble to structure and index project records can improve their accessibility at a future date, when the memory of what has happened is less complete; this makes them much more valuable as a source of reference. Items that can save future effort include:

- copies of templates produced – for the project plan, interviews, questionnaires, updated report forms

- information on how the project was managed

- financial information and reporting

- performance against target

- the project's critical success factors

- skills gaps and the action taken to fill them

- perceptions on what went well and what didn't and what would be done differently next time

- unplanned events and their impact

- team learning from the project.

> **This would be a good time to work through Activity 7.1**

Activity 7.1
Learning from a previous project

Aims of this activity

- to analyse the strengths and weaknesses of a past project
- to identify organisational learning from a past project.

Useful resources for this activity

- *Change, Strategy and Projects at Work*
- Resources at work
- Discussions with colleagues.

1 Identify a completed project in which you were involved or affected by or aware of and which also involved other workplace colleagues.

2 Investigate the strengths and weaknesses of that project by talking to colleagues who were involved and by referring to any reports that are available to you. Where possible, talk through the strengths and weaknesses of the project with colleagues and find out what they think went well and what didn't, asking them to give reasons. Use the following table to make notes about what you discover.

3 Try to identify what was learned from the project by the organisation and the individuals involved and whether learning was systematically captured for future use. Find out whether a project debrief occurred and what methods were used to record what was learned for the benefit of later projects and project teams. If no project debrief occurred is there any evidence of mistakes being repeated in subsequent projects? Note down what you discover in the space provided in the following table.

Title of project:	*Date completed:*
Strengths:	
Weaknesses:	

Learning achieved and recorded:

Further comments from my investigation:

Discussion

At the end of a project there may be pressure to move on to the next challenge, but time spent reflecting on the experience gained in a project can be extremely valuable. When learning is not recognised and recorded for future use, a subsequent project team may find itself having to face problems afresh rather than benefit from previous corporate learning.

8 Learning and looking forward

Throughout this book we have attempted to demystify change, strategy and projects – and wrest these subjects from the grip of specialist managers. We have sought to convince you that these are subjects of relevance to you, in both your working and personal lives, regardless of your current role in the workplace. We hope that you have been encouraged to believe that you can use the knowledge gleaned from this book to help you to analyse change, formulate strategy and implement projects as an instrument of change. Finally, we want you to believe that you can make a positive difference – in your current organisation and throughout your career.

In the world of work today, long held assumptions about job roles and long-term future employability based only upon a one-off experience of specialist training or education in a particular discipline are dead. Future employability will more likely depend upon how well equipped you are to develop your skills of thinking, analysis, communication and learning and how well you can direct them towards achieving personal and organisational goals.

Your current workplace organisation may already be one which aspires to the concept of the learning organisation which we referred to in Chapter 1. Peter Senge[1] describes his view of the learning organisation as places:

where people continually expand their capacity to create the results they truly desire, where new and expansive patterns of thinking are nurtured, where collective aspiration is set free, and where people are continually learning to see the whole (reality) together.

---

[1] Peter Senge Learning Organisation.

In Chapter 7 of this book we have described how, at the end of a project, it is crucial to capture the learning gained from the project process. This would of course apply in equal measure (or even more so) to a complete change programme. Although we haven't assumed that you are currently engaged in carrying out projects within your organisation, or that your organisation is necessarily in a period of transformational change you should be in a better position to apply what you have read to future change situations and be in a stronger position to contribute and possibly influence events for the better.

Having studied this book, you should take the opportunity to critically reflect on the learning that you can take forward with you. To help you do this we have included a final activity based on the employability skills and attributes that employers want their employees to demonstrate and develop. We have focused on skills and attributes that are most closely related to the areas covered in this book, but you will see that many of them are equally valuable assets for any aspect of employment.

This would be a good time to work through Activity 8.1

You may feel uncertain about the skills and attributes that we have suggested are needed, either because you feel that you do not possess them or that you have not had the opportunity to put them to the test – yet. However, a serious attempt at critical reflection on where you believe you now stand and what you should do to develop these skills and attributes for the future would be timely as you conclude your study of this book.

Activity 8.1
Employability skills and attributes

Aim of this activity

◆ To identify and evaluate employability skills and attributes relevant to your workplace.

Useful resources for this activity

◆ *Change, strategy and Projects at Work*

◆ Resources at work

◆ Discussions with colleagues.

The table below that follows sets out twelve categories of employability skills and attributes that are relevant to introducing change through project-based work – though it's by no means a complete list of all employability skills and attributes.

For each skill shown on the list, try to rate your own current level of development by using a number ranging from 1 to 5, 1 being low and 5 being high. Make a note of this in the first of the 'Rating of development' columns. Don't worry if you judge your rating on some of these skills to be low. This is to be expected if you haven't previously worked in situations where you could acquire or build these skills.

The other two 'Rating of development' columns are to enable you to review your development of these skills from time to time.

Employability skills and attributes	Rating of development		
	1 (1–5)	2 (1–5)	3 (1–5)
Written communication:			
Clarity in writing reports and letters, for example, writing for a specified audience			
Ability to explain both simple and complex ideas clearly to a specified audience using written communication			
Ability to read effectively, recognising and retaining key points			
Oral communication:			
Ability to explain both simple and complex ideas clearly to a specified audience using oral communication			
Ability to plan and deliver clear and confident oral presentations to a group			
Ability to listen effectively, recognising and retaining key points			
Teamworking:			
Ability to work constructively with others on a common task			
Ability to resolve conflict through discussion and negotiation to achieve a mutually satisfactory resolution			
Ability to argue or justify a point of view or a course of action			
Leadership:			
Ability to motivate, encourage, direct and support others in the achievement of specific objectives			
Ability to manage and implement change			
Confidence and willingness to accept ultimate responsibility			

Interpersonal skills:				
Ability to relate well to other people				
Ability to work cross-culturally, both within and beyond your organisation				
Sensitivity to other's emotions and appreciation of the effects that they can have				
Computer literacy:				
Ability to use a range of commercial software such as word processing and spreadsheet applications				
Ability to use and manage computer communication tools such as email, instant messaging, blogging				
Ability to use a computer to access, store and manage information				
Numeracy:				
Ability to interpret and work with numerical information in the form of charts, graphs, statistics, fractions and percentages				
Ability to perform accurately basic arithmetic calculations such as addition, subtraction, multiplication and division				
Ability to prepare estimates and work with budgets				
Planning and organisation:				
Ability to work in an efficient and structured manner				
Ability to rank tasks according to importance				
Ability to set achievable goals and produce a plan of action to reach those goals				
Initiative:				
Ability to work without supervision, make decisions and take unprompted action				

Employability skills and attributes	Rating of development		
	1 (1–5)	2 (1–5)	3 (1–5)
Problem solving:			
Ability to handle ambiguous and complex situations			
Ability to analyse a problem or situation			
Ability to select and use appropriate methods to find solutions to problems			
Ability to choose the best option from a range of alternatives			
Ability to be original or inventive and to apply creative thinking			
Adaptability/flexibility:			
Ability to respond positively to changing circumstances and new challenges			
Commitment to ongoing learning to meet the needs of employment			
Ability to retain effectiveness under pressure			
Effectiveness in an organisation:			
Disposition to engage with reflective evaluation of the performance of yourself and others			
Ability to recognise and develop your strengths and to recognise and overcome your weaknesses			
Understanding of organisational strategic objectives and business processes			
Ongoing awareness of your organisation's external and internal context			
An understanding of your role within the organisational context			
Ability to foster mutually beneficial professional relationships			
Ability to access various information sources and to select and critique information			
Appreciation of ethical aspects of employment and ability to act morally and with integrity			

Discussion

Don't forget, as well as self-assessment, you can also use evidence from appraisals, work you have undertaken during which you may have demonstrated these skills and attributes, and feedback you have received from others. If you feel self-confident enough, you could also ask the opinions of trusted colleagues and friends to gain other perspectives. Above all, be honest with yourself – and if you do identify development needs (which you surely will) be prepared to take action to meet them.

Appendix: Techniques for problem solving and decision making

Brainstorming

There are many adaptations of brainstorming. This technique can be productive in developing new perspectives to overcome problem areas. In its basic form, it is a group activity best conducted away from the interruptions of the normal workplace environment. The benefits arise from the generation of ideas from a variety of people. The process needs careful facilitation.

If possible, provide material to start people thinking about the problem area some days before the session is to be carried out. The sub-conscious mind can produce new insights in the absence of conscious effort.

Plan how the session will be structured, first to revisit the problem area and then to encourage brief suggestions from others. An icebreaker activity can help people to feel at ease and create a non-threatening atmosphere where participants feel safe and less inhibited. Record ideas as people state them, without adding meaning.

Judgement on ideas put forward should be deferred as criticism can constrain further suggestions; some apparently silly ideas can lead to useful new perspectives on a problem. Ideas should be sought from all participants, not allowing a few to dominate the proceedings.

Summarise and record the outcomes of the brainstorming session, so that these can be fed back to all those concerned. People may make additional suggestions or develop some of the ideas further as they review the outcomes. A follow up meeting is normally required soon afterwards to decide on the way forward.

Ishikawa/fishbone diagram

Often when a problem arises there is a focus on symptoms rather than cause. Identifying the true cause of a problem is necessary before an effective solution can be proposed.

One useful tool for identifying the causes of problems is a fishbone diagram – so called because it resembles the skeleton of a fish. It is also known as a cause and effect diagram, because it provides a systematic way of working from effects – what is actually happening – to the originating or contributory causes. It can be used to explore a problem area where things are going wrong and yet it is not clear why. The usefulness of the method is dependent upon the quality of the brainstorming accompanying the process. In the construction of a fishbone diagram it is important to focus first on causes

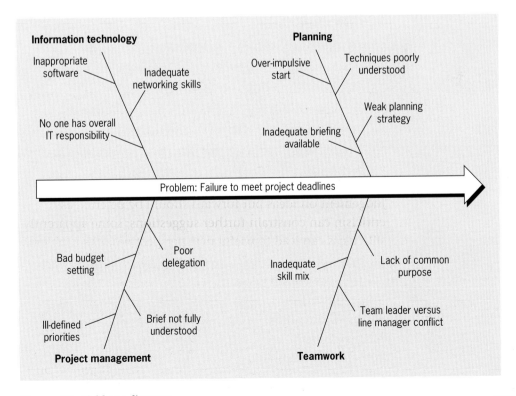

Figure A1 *Fishbone diagram*

Source: *Tyler (2004)*

rather than solutions. Where causes recur further examination may be particularly rewarding (Figure A1).

The stages in constructing a fishbone diagram are:

1. First, define the problem for which the causes must be identified, for example, packages delivered late.

2. Draw a thick horizontal arrow, (representing the spine of a fish) with arrow pointing to the right. Label the arrow with the problem.

3. Brainstorm the major categories of possible causes. Some typical examples are:
   - the four Ms: Methods, Machines, Materials, Manpower
   - the four Ps: Place, Procedures, People, Provisions
   - the four Ss: Surroundings, Suppliers, Systems, Skills.

4. Draw thinner subsidiary bones for each of these main categories, pointing in towards the spine at an angle of about 45 degrees.

5. For each main category, brainstorm each possible cause, adding any identified factors to the diagram as progressively thinner subsidiary bones.

6. The procedure is repeated until it is agreed that all possible root causes have been identified.

7. From all possible causes the most likely root cause is identified.

Nominal group technique

Another more formal approach to problem solving is the nominal group technique. This involves all the members of a group and seeks consensus to evaluate and rank all the ideas generated. It is very democratic, as its outcome is a group agreement about what action is required to solve the problem. The steps are:

1. The team leader presents the problem (or opportunity) to the group, without suggesting a preferred solution.

2. Working on their own, everyone writes down a list of potential solutions.

3. Everyone, in turn, reports just one of their ideas. Each idea is recorded on a flip chart without initial comment and without recording the originator's name

4. The group has a brief discussion to clarify ideas and, provided owners agree, to amalgamate similar ones.

5. Each member of the group individually identifies their 'top 5' ideas in order of preference, communicating this directly to the group leader without discussion.

6. The leader generates a 'top 5' group list from the individual lists and this is communicated back to the group for discussion.

7. Finally, a vote is taken to identify the preferred idea(s).

Source: *Baguley* (1999).

Six Thinking Hats technique

Many heads are frequently better than one when faced with problems in need of a decision, but in practice, group discussions can become unstructured. People are likely to approach a problem area from different directions, take opposing positions, argue and talk at cross-purposes. Although a decision may have been taken and the discussion moves on, some may feel a sense of unease. Were all the aspects of a problem explored fully? Is the decision the right one?

The Six Thinking Hats technique, developed by Edward de Bono (1985), is a simple way of slowing down thinking and making it explicit. It is based on the idea that there are six distinct categories of thinking – such as being creative and being judgemental – and that thinking is most constructive if group members are able to focus all thinking energies on one category of thinking at a time. The six categories of thinking are each represented by a metaphorical coloured hat.

The technique depends on everyone conforming to a mode of thinking signalled by the colour of a (normally) imaginary hat. This encourages people to think along parallel lines in a supportive rather than confrontational way, but still retaining the advantage of building ideas based upon a variety of perspectives.

The Six Thinking Hats are specified as:

White hat	facts and information – known or needed
Black hat	logical, judgemental and cautious – why an idea or a proposal may not work
Yellow hat	positive, optimistic and logical – why an idea will work and the benefits it brings
Red hat	feelings, emotions, intuitions – without having to justify them
Green hat	creativity, possibilities, options, new ideas
Blue hat	procedural – thinking about the process that is underway

The colour of the hat gives a direction to the discussion but the direction of the discussion can be changed by the group chair. For example, 'That's good white hat thinking. Let's do some green hat thinking for a while'. This means that having focused on the information that participants can bring to the discussion, the discussion can now switch to generate and consider new ideas.

de Bono argues that Six Hats thinking can make meetings more productive and save time. It helps everyone to combine their knowledge, intelligence and expertise and work together with greater synergy.

Plan–Do–Check–Act or PDCA cycle

Although project tasks are set out in a linear sequence – start at A and end at B – much of the monitoring and review process is iterative and cyclical: returning to review an action or problem before moving forward (Figure A2).

The Plan–Do–Check–Act or PDCA cycle was developed in the 1930s as a tool for achieving continuous improvement.

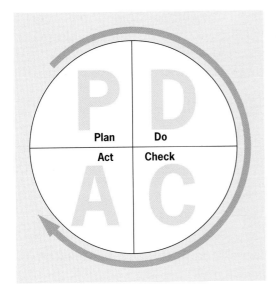

Figure A2 *The PDCA cycle*

Source: *Adapted from HCi (www)*

It stresses the cyclical nature of improvement programmes, beginning with planning and resulting in effective action. This is what each stage of the cycle involves:

Plan: Find out which things are going wrong and come up with ideas for solving the problems.

Do: Implement changes designed to solve the problems on a small or experimental scale first to minimise disruption to routine work, whether the changes work or not.

Check: Whether these changes are achieving the desired result.

Act: Implement changes on a larger scale if the experiment is successful. Also act to involve other people; for example, project stakeholders who are affected by the changes and whose co-operation is needed to implement them on a larger scale, or those who may simply benefit from what has been learned.

If the experiment was not successful, skip the Act stage and go back to Plan to come up with alternative ideas for solving the problem and commence the cycle again.

If the problem is a complex one, it may benefit from using some formal problem-solving techniques at the Plan stage. The following suggestions to help structure and support decision making are adapted from Mcdonald (1999):

1. Be clear what the problem is – check facts before reacting.

2. Is the problem unique? If not, see if previous problem-solving decisions would work now.

3. Does the problem require just one (right or wrong) decision or is it a matter of choosing the best of several options?

4. Consider a group brainstorming session: even an off-the-wall idea might spark a useful line of thought.

5. Consult those who may have had experience of the same problem.

6. Make sure there is enough information to support a proper decision.

7. Where appropriate apply critical path analysis techniques to eliminate those options that are impractical or otherwise unacceptable.

8. Make sure that information is reliable and up to date – has the person who gathered it sufficient experience, been given sufficient time and based their investigation on correct assumptions?

9. Where possible, allow some time for thoughts to clarify before finalising a decision.

Paired comparisons

This technique is useful for preparing a ranked order of options when considering ideas, criteria, preferences and so on, up to a maximum of about 15 items. As the number of items increases so does the size of table needed to compare pairs; but computer aided methods can help.

A table of size $n \times n$ is required, where n is the number of items to be compared. Label the top row and left hand column in the manner shown in the Table A1, noting that an item will not need comparing with itself.

Where columns and rows intersect compare pairs of options and using suitable shorthand identify which of the pair is preferred. The symbol $>$ is used to indicate 'better than'. Three asterisks express very much preferred, two asterisks express moderately preferred and one asterisk, slightly preferred.

Total the number of asterisks that express the preference for each option to produce the preferred list in rank order.

Table A1 *Paired comparisons for a selection of vegetables*

	Cabbage(c)	Leeks(l)	Onions(o)	Parsnips(p)	Sprouts(s)
Beans(b)	b > c**	l > b*	b > o**	p > b*	b > s**
Cabbage		l > c***	c > o*	p > c***	s > c*
Leeks			l > o**	l > p*	l > s*
Onions				p > o*	s > o*
Parsnips					p > s***

Ranked preferences:

Leeks 8*, parsnips 8*, beans 6*, sprouts 2*, cabbage 1*, onions 0*.

Comparison tables

Comparison tables may be used to compare a limited number of options using weightings to express the importance of perceived benefits or attributes. The example in Table A2 compares alternative options for maintaining fitness. A table can be constructed by:

1. First, options are listed in the left hand column of a table.

2. Next those criteria that are perceived to be important are listed in the top row cells.

3. Each criterion is carefully weighted to indicate its importance; for example, 1 lowest, 3 highest importance.

4. Each option is scored in terms of each criterion, for example, between 1 (low) and 5 (high).

5. Each score is multiplied by the weighting factor.

6. The weighted scores are totalled to determine the highest weighted score – in this case, running.

In the example shown, the weighted score for running suggests that this would be the optimal strategy for keeping fit based upon the expressed preferences and criteria.

Table A2 *Weighted comparison table for fitness strategies*

Criteria	Flexibility		Cost		Social		Time spent		Total
Relative weighting	3		1		2		3		
Alternative strategies	Raw score	Weighted ×3	Raw score	Weighted ×1	Raw score	Weighted ×2	Raw score	Weighted ×3	Weighted score
Running	3	9	5	5	2	4	3	9	27
Walking	4	12	5	5	1	2	1	3	22
Cycling	2	6	4	4	1	2	2	6	18
Fitness club	2	6	1	1	4	8	2	6	21
Swimming	1	3	2	2	2	4	3	9	18

Pareto analysis

Pareto was an 18th century economist who observed that 80% of wealth in his city was held by 20% of the population. The so-called 80/20 rule is encountered quite frequently; for example, a business may find that 80% of its sales comes from roughly 20% of its customers. When faced with solving a problem in the workplace you may find that 80% of a problem's impact can be removed by attending to 20% of the identified, contributory causes. This means that if the most significant causes (20%) can be identified and dealt with as a priority, then the most significant part of the problem (80%) can be eliminated.

The approach in a Pareto analysis is to identify and list the possible factors or categories that are contributing to the perceived problem area and to rank them using a scoring mechanism.

First the problem facing the organisation is articulated then all the relevant contributory factors or categories relating to the problem are listed. Next a scoring system to quantify the significance of each factor (e.g. score out of 10) is devised and applied. Next, the highest-scored fifth of possible factors is identified. These factors are prioritised for problem solving and then action.

Note that when this process has been completed and the problem area reduced, the 80/20 rule is still likely to apply in that 80% of the remaining problem is likely to be attributable to 20% of the remaining contributory factors.

Decision-tree analysis

A decision-tree diagram can be used to represent a situation where different decisions are possible and can help with analysing the consequences of making one decision rather than another. Decision trees can be used in different ways. Whilst they are used in quite complex decision-making algorithms in software and management applications, they can also be used to analyse all possible routes through a decision-making process and to quantify the risks associated with sequences of events that relate to particular decisions.

In Figure A3 decision points are represented by small squares. Events that occur after taking a particular decision are shown using chance nodes, represented by small circles. A sequence of events is represented by linked chance nodes. Each event at each chance node should be assessed and given a probability value, to express the likelihood of its occurrence. All possible events should be represented and the probabilities at each chance node should add up to 1. Note that a probability of 0 represents an event which is a complete impossibility, whilst a probability of 1 represents an event which is certain to happen. All other probability values lie between these two extremes and represent various degrees of certainty.

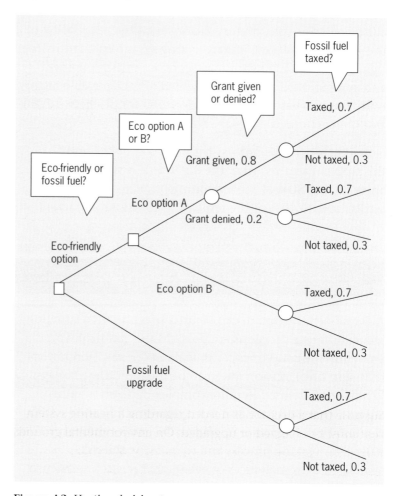

Figure A3 *Heating decision tree*

The likelihood of sequences of events linked by branches through more than one chance node, can normally be expressed (provided the events are statistically independent) by multiplying out the individual probabilities as shown in the Table A3. Even the act of simply drawing out a decision tree showing the various options for decision making can help to clarify a complex situation. For a meaningful analysis though, care must be taken to ensure that probability values ascribed to events are realistic. Working through the scenario associated with Figure A3 will help you to understand the process.

Table A3 *Routes through the heating system decision tree*

Following Figure A3 and working from left to right and top to bottom:					
Decision node	Decision node	Chance node	Chance node	Likelihood of this happening	Viable?
Eco-friendly option	Eco option A	Grant given (0.8)	Fossil fuel taxed (0.7)	$0.8 \times 0.7 = 0.56$	Yes
Eco-friendly option	Eco option A	Grant given (0.8)	Fossil fuel not taxed (0.3)	$0.8 \times 0.3 = 0.24$	Yes
Eco-friendly option	Eco option A	Grant denied (0.2)	Fossil fuel taxed (0.7)	$0.2 \times 0.7 = 0.14$	No
Eco-friendly option	Eco option A	Grant denied (0.2)	Fossil fuel not taxed (0.3)	$0.2 \times 0.3 = 0.06$	Yes
Eco-friendly option	Eco option B	Fossil fuel taxed (0.7)		0.7	No
Eco-friendly option	Eco option B	Fossil fuel not taxed (0.3)		0.3	Yes
Fossil fuel upgrade	Fossil fuel taxed (0.7)			0.7	No
Fossil fuel upgrade	Fossil fuel not taxed (0.3)			0.3	Yes

Scenario for the decision tree

Suppose that a decision is needed regarding a heating system that must be changed or upgraded. On environmental grounds it would be good to choose an eco-friendly system, rather than simply upgrade the existing fossil fuel (electric) heating system, but what are the risks and financial implications?

Imagine for the purpose of this example that one of the eco-friendly options would be eligible for a grant, provided that a required level of performance can be attained. Another uncertainty stems from proposed legislation to impose a 20% tax on fossil fuels. This may or may not be implemented. Both of the eco-friendly options would be affected because they use a significant amount of electricity to function. The fossil fuel option would only be financially viable if the proposal for a fossil fuel tax fails. Figure A3 represents the situation described, though in practice additional factors may need to be included.

Working through the permutations associated with the scenario, Table A3 shows all possible outcomes from Figure A3. Examining these should help you decide whether, for your (or your organisation's) current financial situation, it would be wise and justifiable to choose the eco-friendly options. What is the likelihood of the events following a decision working out favourably? The information given to guide your decision is that:

Eco-friendly option A would be viable if the grant application is successful, whether or not the fossil fuel tax is implemented.

Eco-friendly option A would also be viable if the grant application is denied but only if the fossil fuel tax proposal failed.

Eco-friendly option B would be viable only if the fossil fuel tax proposal failed.

The fossil fuel upgrade would be viable only if the fossil fuel tax proposal failed.

Looking at the probabilities associated with each of these branches could help to make the right decision under conditions of uncertainty.

For the three viable branches associated with eco option A, the likelihood of this choice being successful can be expressed by adding the calculated probability values associated with each sequence happening; that is 0.56 + 0.24 + 0.06 = 0.86, which provides a high level of confidence associated with choosing eco option A. Choosing eco option B or the fossil fuel upgrade, in either case there is only a 0.3 likelihood of this being financially viable.

Although this scenario simplifies the basis for the best overall decision, it does show how a decision tree can assist with a decision-making process.

References

Baguley, P. (1999). *Project Management*, Hodder.

Bronfenbrenner, U. (1979). The Ecology of Human Development: Experiment by Nature and Design, Harvard University Press, USA.

Bruce, A. and Langdon, K. (2000). *Project management*, Dorling Kindersley.

Carnall, C. (1999). *Managing Change in Organisations* (2nd edition), Financial Times Prentice Hall, London, UK.

de Bono, E. (1985). *Six Thinking Hats*, Little, Brown and Company USA.

JISC infoNet Project Management www.jiscinfonet.ac.uk

Johnson, G. and Scholes, K. (1999). *Exploring Corporate Strategy* (2nd edition), Prentice Hall, Europe.

Lake, C. (1997). *Mastering Project Management: Key Skills in Ensuring Profitable and Successful Projects*, Thorogood, London, UK.

Luecke, R. and Katz, R. (2003). *Managing Creativity and Innovation*, Harvard Business School Press, Boston, MA, ISBN 1-59139-112-1.

Mcdonald, J. (1999). *Project Management*, Croner.

Paton, R. and McCalman, J. (2000). *Change Management: A Guide to Effective Implementation* (2nd edition), SAGE Publications, London, UK.

Santayana, G. (1905–1906). *The Life of Reason: Or, The Phases of Human Progress*, 5 vols. Available free online from Project Gutenberg, 1998, 1 vol. abridgement by the author and Daniel Cory. Prometheus Books.

Senge, P. (1992). *The Fifth Discipline: The Art and Practice of the Learning Organization*, Doubleday, New York, USA.

References

Stacey, R. (1996). *Strategic Management and Organizational Dynamics* (2nd edition), Pitman, London.

Tuckman, B. and Jenson, M. (1977). Stages of small group development revisited. *Groups and Organisation Studies*, 2, 419–427.

Tyler, S. (2004). *The Manager's Good Study Guide*, The Open University, Milton Keynes, UK.

http://encyclopedia.thefreedictionary.com/ Meredith + Belbin

http://encyclopedia.thefreedictionary.com/Praxis + (process)

http://www.prince2passport.com/SPOCE_Mini_Method_V3/ PMGuide.html

http://www.prince2passport.com/SPOCE_Mini_Method_V3/ PMGuide.html

www.belbin.com

Index

213